CHRISTIAN FOUNDATIONS

ROME AND REFORMATION

A STUBBORN PROBLEM RE-EXAMINED

by

JAMES ATKINSON

HODDER AND STOUGHTON

First printed 1966

Printed in Great Britain for Hodder and Stoughton Limited,
St. Paul's House, Warwick Lane, London, E.C.4,
by Hazell Watson & Viney Ltd, Aylesbury, Bucks

INTRODUCTION

TODAY it is no longer fashionable to speak in terms of 'controversy' but rather of 'conversation', and this is all to the good. It is undoubtedly better for old adversaries to speak *to* each other rather than *against* each other, and for those who (though in separation) profess the name of Christ to regard each other with charity. But a change of attitude, however welcome, does not necessarily imply a radical change of situation, and it would be unhelpful to suggest that it did.

The differences between Protestantism and Roman Catholicism are real differences. They concern vital issues in defence of which men have been willing to lay down their lives. Rome and the Reformation still stand over against each other in such a way that, if reunion is to be achieved, either Protestantism must recant the distinctive doctrines of the Reformation, or Roman Catholicism must retract the anathemas of Trent (pronounced against those doctrines) and be open to reform, in root as well as in branches, in submission to the authority of the Word of God.

This should not be taken to imply that Protestantism is not in need of reform—it is desperately so; its prevailing state of doctrinal incoherence can hardly be impressive or attractive to others. The very best thing that could happen would be for both 'sides' to sit down together—preferably in small, informal groups—and humbly, patiently, expectantly, and without prejudice (which can only come about by the grace of

God) to study the source-book of our faith, the New Testament of our Lord and Saviour Jesus Christ.

Canon James Atkinson has the advantage of being a theologian with a specialized knowledge of the theological conflict of the sixteenth century, as well as being a student of the exceptionally interesting developments of our own day. What he says in the pages that follow is marked by freshness, charity, and an eirenic spirit. As a contribution to the contemporary debate it will do much to clarify a situation which is not always free from confusion.

PHILIP E. HUGHES

FRANK COLQUHOUN

Joint Editors

CONTENTS

Part One

WHAT THE REFORMATION
WAS ABOUT

1. MOTIVATED BY SCHOLARLY, RESPONSIBLE THEOLOGIANS AND CHURCHMEN

RIGHTEOUS, scholarly, committed Christian men of the stature of Luther, Calvin, Bucer, and Zwingli—to say nothing of our own Latimer, Cranmer, Ridley—do not easily turn against the Church which bred them and fed them. To understand the Reformation we must understand the deep religious concern which motivated these men, and why it was that the sixteenth-century Church compelled them at great cost reluctantly to wear the mantle of reformer cast upon them by opponents. They were anathematized and excommunicated by the Church, opposed and outlawed by the Empire; yet their theology has never been rebutted nor their arguments answered. The cost of their witness was a divided—and therefore debilitated—Christendom. When Hans Küng writes that the Vatican Council is four hundred years too late, and the pope actually says that the Roman Church must take some blame for the break-up of Christendom, we have heard for the first time in four centuries an admission that could never be wrung out of the Roman Church before today. All that the Reformers asked for was for a representative ecumenical council to go into the malaise of Christendom. The request was never granted. The council has not since materialized. The need is as urgent today as when Luther called on the responsible laity in 1520 to impose such a council on an unwilling Church.

It was the refusal of the Church to reform her theology and mend her morals, and restore both to the pattern taught by Christ and the apostles, that made half of Christendom turn a deaf ear to Rome and cleave to the Reformers. What is wholly new in the present situation is that Pope John, in calling the Roman Catholic Church to his new policy of *aggiornamento*, had called it not only to set its own house in order but to relate itself positively to other communions as well as to the world. There is now, therefore, a very genuine debate going on at all levels, and this book is a small contribution to that discussion. It seems to the writer important to re-consider those issues on which in Reformation days good Christian men in the name of Christ would not capitulate, and to ask again why a large part of the Church of the sixteenth century would not reform itself theologically. The writer does not wish to raise again dead issues of the sixteenth century, such as a discussion on usury, nor fight battles of long ago, as for example concerning the ubiquity of the Lord's body. He seeks to look steadily and whole at the total religious concern of the Reformation, and to invite Roman Catholics and Anglo-Catholics to look again at this cause to see whether or not its fundamental concerns were right, and whether, in the light of truths which both sides are concerned to uphold, a new and larger way forward may under God be vouchsafed to us all.

The writer is a thorough-going Anglican, who sees in historic Anglicanism less a compromise than a stroke of genius. The Church of England is the reformed catholic Church of this realm, securely founded on Scripture, broad catholic tradition, and sound reason. Anglicanism is different from Roman Catholicism, as it is different from the Free Church position. True Anglicanism seeks, fallibly, to preserve all that was pure and sound in historic Catholicism, as well as all the evangelical impulses of the Reformation. An Anglican is peculiarly fitted to investigate the issues of the Reformation, for his whole outlook is characterized by respect and regard for catholic tradition, a deep concern for Scripture, and the desire to follow the argument wherever sound reason and scholarship lead it. Further, the writer has no partisan approach; he teaches academic theology in a university constituted of all persuasions, and teaches ecumenical theology to a voluntarily constituted class consisting of Roman Catholic priests and nuns, as well as Roman Catholic, Anglican, and Free Church laity.

2. A MOVEMENT WITHIN A VORTEX OF SOCIAL, CULTURAL, AND ECONOMIC REVOLUTIONS

Before we examine the fundamental concerns of the Reformation we ought to remind ourselves that the Reformation was a religious movement within a vortex of other movements. We cannot examine these here but we must mention them.

It was the day of the great sailors and voyagers, when men like Columbus and Cabot were bringing back evidence of a new world, and men like Copernicus were explaining that the sun, not the Earth, was the centre of the universe. Further, the Renaissance had gained great strength, and its thinkers had begun to harvest the fruits of a rejuvenated scholarship which laughed at the follies of the friars and the subtleties of the scholastics, and supplied the Reformers with adequate texts of Scripture and the Fathers, together with an academic discipline empowering them to use them. The Reformers were hardly men of the Renaissance, but they used perfectly the tools provided by Renaissance scholarship. The political scene too was fluid. Francis I schemed against Charles V, helped occasionally by the pope. The Turk was knocking at the gates of Vienna. The states of Germany were seeking autonomy from the Emperor and relief of papal taxation from Rome. The old aristocratic order was dying and its feudalism everywhere giving place to a robust capitalism. The lot of the peasant was deteriorating alarmingly, while, through economic pressures which nobody at the time understood, prices were rising everywhere. It was in this vast turmoil of movements—intellectual, political, social, cultural—that the Reformation was born. In many places and in the minds of many people, the theological Reformation became involved with, and sometimes corrupted by, or even prostituted to, one or more of these movements. It is therefore important to distinguish what exactly the Reformation meant, and not to confuse it with socialism, humanism, or any other secular ideology.

If the Reformation has not to be confused with its contemporary political, social and intellectual movements, though it cannot be dissociated from them, nor has it to be thought of as merely a movement to abolish scandal and immorality in the Church. Luther's first concern was not with scandal but with theology. 'Others, who have lived before me, have attacked the pope's evil and scandalous life; but I have attacked his doctrine.' In discussing Huss, Luther said, 'John Huss attacked and castigated only the pope's abuses and scandalous life; but I . . . have attacked the pope's doctrine and overthrown him.' In fact Luther always distinguished himself from other and earlier reformers of the Church in that they had always sought to tidy up the scandals and abuses whereas his sole concern was for an evangelical theology. This is our key, in fact the only key, to the Reformation.

3. WHAT WERE THE THEOLOGICAL PRINCIPLES OF THE REFORMATION?

These can best be seen in Luther, in that Luther's evangelical theology brought about the Reformation and was, with certain modifications, taken into the system of all those parts of the Church which reformed themselves: Germany, Switzerland, France, the Netherlands, Denmark, Norway, Sweden, England and Scotland.

SALVATION IN CHRIST ALONE APART FROM WORKS AND MERIT

Salvation by free unmerited grace in Christ is, of course, a truth basic to any and all interpretations of Christianity. There was nothing new here. There was in fact nothing new in Luther's theology at all, yet that theology made everything new. Why? The Church had had critics of her theology and criticisms of her morality for centuries. Why was it then that Luther's heart was kindled to such heat as to warm the chilled heart of Christendom?

The answer to that question is most conveniently expressed in Luther's controversy with Erasmus on the *Bondage of the Will* (1525). Erasmus had long advised the Church against precipitate action with regard to Luther, and when the effects of Luther's theology were realized, Erasmus was goaded into an attack on Luther lest he himself be condemned as a sympathizer. Erasmus was in fact a reformer of a kind, and a biting critic of the theology and practices of his day, but he never wanted more than the removal of scandals and a simplification of Christianity in accordance with the teaching of Christ. Erasmus very cleverly attacked the Lutheran theology on the Pauline and Augustinian doctrine of the will enslaved to self. Luther realized that Erasmus had not deigned to consider the matter of indulgences and other petty scandals, but had gone to the heart of Luther's Gospel. Erasmus had 'grabbed him by the throat', as he expressed it.

This is the real issue of the Reformation: it concerns the nature and content of the Gospel. On the one hand there is the Gospel interpreted by Erasmus, the Christian scholar and man of letters, and, on the other hand, the Gospel experienced by Luther the theologian and man of God. Luther saw that man's salvation lay utterly, wholly and only in the free sovereign grace of God; that the natural man lay fast bound in sin, and that the faith which received Christ was itself a free gift of a merciful God which raised him into a new life in the act of effectual calling. The refined and sensitive Erasmus believed that despite the fall man was essentially good, at any rate good enough to know what was good and to respond to the good: he believed that by his own efforts and discipline he could attain some fellowship with God and make himself acceptable to God. Erasmus thought of salvation in terms of what man could do to respond to what God had done. Luther, however, had discovered that by doing everything that lay in him he was no nearer to God at all, and this had led him to realize that salvation lay wholly in God's work, not at all in man's. Erasmus's theology was an anthropology: Luther's theology a Christology.

This truth needs sharpening, for it divides evangelical theology from all other religious systems, catholic, moralist, humanist, judaistic alike. Long before any break with Rome, as early as 1512, in his *Lectures on the Psalms* (1513–15), and clearly argued in his *Lectures on the Epistle to the Romans* (1515), years before the indulgences controversy, Luther reiterated this truth with crystal clarity. To Luther, God had shown his hand in Christ. He used to tell his students it was not a matter of what they thought about God and how they looked at Him but how God thought towards them and looked at them, a revelation they could know only in Christ. In Christ God had done all He could do for man.

'Here God pours out not sun or moon, nor heaven and earth, but His own heart and his dearest Son, and even suffers Him to shed His blood and die the most shameful of all deaths for us shameful, wicked, ungrateful, people.' (WA.36.426.34ff.)

Here was the central fault of the Christianity of his day, a fault in which as a monk he was more sunk than any man. Monkery was but a long discipline of works and efforts whereby a man sought to grow nearer to God: Luther found this long discipline drove him into a hellish awareness of his own sin and of his ultimate condemnation. Mysticism sought to cultivate in him the presence of God: Luther realized that there was no ascent to God from below. Academic theology was little more than a speculation on the nature of God and His attributes: Luther realized that the outcome of such intellectualism was to produce an idol. All these techniques had this one error in common: ultimately they trusted in man's own morality, his own intellect, his own spirituality, to get him to God, or at least near enough for God to accept him. Luther realized that it was not a matter of God being far from man and man having to strive to attain Him, but that the reverse was true. It was man in his creatureliness and sin who was far from God, and it was God in Christ who had come all the way to find him. This, of course, was an old truth, but it had been overlaid. It was indeed the treasure hid in a field. To believe in the power of man to effect his own salvation, even in part, even to start it off, even to further it, was (and to some extent still is) the heresy of Rome. Luther called this '*hominem praedicare*', 'to preach man'.

From this error came the ruin of the Church, and still comes the ruin of the Church. It is not only an error of Roman Catholic theology, but, with much less excuse, Liberal Protestant theology has taught the same error from another direction. All the excesses of the medieval church—for example, monkery as a 'higher' Christian life, pilgrimages and disciplines—took their root here. It was only when Luther diagnosed the malaise of Christendom in his own soul that he could offer the saving truth of the Gospel; or rather, that the saving truth of the Gospel was revealed to him, to offer again to his Church. Luther had tried all the medieval practices to make himself good enough to be acceptable to God. When all his efforts were of no avail, he realized that basically he was relying on himself and his works, and that this was not Christian faith. His anthropocentric cry, 'Oh when will you only be pious and do sufficient to find a gracious God?' returned an empty echo, and in that emptiness God spoke in Christ: 'It is not of him that willeth, nor of him that runneth, but of God that sheweth mercy.'

In his early years at the monastery Luther believed that he was wrestling with his sin. In actual fact he was struggling with the religion of his day and the Church's technique and doctrine of salvation. The Church over the centuries had gradually lapsed into a doctrine of salvation based essentially on merit and works. It was in Luther's day less a matter of God and His work, more a matter of man and his works. Therefore it came to be less a matter of faith in God and more a matter of trust in works, disciplines, practices. Faith to the contemporaries of Luther was essentially assent to doctrines, or perhaps opinions about God, and confidence in the teaching and practices of the Church. At root it was essentially a human effort to know God and to understand Him. It was here that Luther broke away. Valid as this kind of faith might be, it was not what the New Testament meant by faith nor how Luther had come to understand it. To him faith was a living assurance of a God who had shown His hand in Christ. It meant no faith in ourselves or our disciplines and efforts at all, but a total recognition of our own frailty, our creatureliness, our finitude, our sin, in answer to which God of His mercy had given Christ for us men and for our salvation, and then called us to an unwavering faith in Himself.

It was this impulse of Christianity (that man was saved by Christ alone and not at all by his own works and efforts no matter how genuinely and christianly intended) that was the mainspring of the Reformation. Reform followed everywhere, England included, not by the organizing and planning activity of men seeking to improve things, but by the touch of God in the hearts and minds of men of faith. It is an experience rather than a doctrine, a way of life rather than a theory, an event rather than an idea. No man can utter one syllable of sense about God until God has talked to him, and declared His election of him in Christ by His free unmerited mercy. Luther proclaimed this Gospel rather than argued it, as the apostles before him. Paul could only begin, as he said, 'When it pleased God to reveal His Son in me . . .' Luther began then. We begin there too.

There was certainly nothing new in Luther's theology. What was new was a fresh experience of God in Christ. It was from that certain experience, wholly different in kind from the medieval idea of earning salvation by merit and ecclesiastical 'good works', that the whole heart of Europe was strangely warmed. What Luther was talking about, as was the New Testament, was the encounter of God with a believing man, not man's efforts to find Him.

Perhaps an Anglo-Catholic or a Roman Catholic reading these words might be disposed to say that salvation in Christ only, free and unmerited, is basic to his theology too. Then we are already at one, and at one in Christ. Nevertheless, the writer suggests that though it is believed in, it is believed in with certain modifications. The Catholic (even the Liberal Protestant, sometimes the average Christian, sometimes the high Anglican, always the natural man) makes room beside all this for his own co-operation, his own discipline, his own efforts, and his own works alongside. Though all of these may be intrinsically good and desirable in their own place, yet they are wrong when regarded as meritorious, and therefore to place them alongside the free, unmerited grace of God means, in effect, to modify the principle and not basically to believe in it. If a cook makes a cake with fat as well as eggs it is because he knows it is better with both. This is essentially the Catholic view: both faith and works. The abuses and scandals largely disappeared with the Council of Trent but the theology remained the same, and in some respects has hardened.

THE REPLACEMENT OF A MEDIATORIAL PRIESTHOOD BY THE PRIESTHOOD OF ALL BELIEVERS

(2)

It took Luther some years to regain the central New Testament affirmation of salvation in Christ alone, and to restate its truth in relation to his study of Scripture and church history. He never for a moment thought he had discovered anything, but rather that the essential nature of the New Testament Gospel had been vouchsafed to him, and with that the power to see Roman Catholic tradition steadily and whole. His study of the Epistle to the Romans had convinced him that salvation was not in man but God, not of him that willeth nor of him that runneth but of God who showeth mercy (Rom. 9 : 16). He then realized, what countless Christians had always realized down the centuries, that with all his intellect and with all his do-it-yourself efforts after spirituality, he was getting nowhere. He grew painfully aware of the worthlessness of all the auxiliary activities which had gained currency in his day: monasticism, fasting, pilgrimages, expiations, good works, ascetic practices, and all the rest. If God had opened His heart in Christ and revealed Himself to man reconciling lost man to Himself while yet in sin (2 Cor. 5 : 19, Rom. 5 : 8), then this truth had only to be stated to be seen. It was not the seeing of it but the declaration of it to the Church of his day that caused the disturbance and hostility. This truth presented to the world had once converted the world: when presented to a sinful Church she turned on the man who proclaimed it to her with all the venom associated usually with an enemy.

If a man knows the truth of salvation in Christ alone there is no place in his life for a mediatorial or sacrificing priest. Medieval Christians believed that the life of the soul was created, nourished and perfected through sacramental grace, of which the priest was the sole purveyor. Pardon was the word of the priest given (sometimes withheld), not the repentance and forgiveness proclaimed by Christ. Grace was a kind of spiritual medicine the priest dispensed, not the personal relationship of the New Testament. The keys of heaven were keys on the girdle of the priest, not the promise of being in Christ.

Rumblings of this liberation had already been heard in England in the fourteenth century. The Englishman was less concerned about papal exactions, which he hardly experienced in that they were not directed against the commonalty but rather against high ecclesiastics and kings, but he was concerned about the property and possessions of his own clergy. Towards the end of the fourteenth century there were already serious outbursts of religious and social discontent. As long as the centre of the power of the priesthood was the mass, as long as the priest alone was recognized as able to offer this sacrifice and call down the mysterious presence of the Saviour Himself, upon whom the salvation of the world depended, great indeed was the power of the priest, and all the greater for being mysterious and only partly understood. Once this belief in the mass as a saving sacrifice is removed, the priest ceases to be the only possible mediator with heaven, and is compelled to stand as a plain minister to a congregation. The popular attack concentrated, therefore, in seeking to change this mass into a holy communion, and to dispel the belief that by his words the priest converted the bread and wine into the very body and blood of Christ. It was with our own movement under Wycliffe that the layman sought to cut the priest down to size. The Reformation really first directed itself against the mass not against Rome.

But Luther delved more deeply into the history and theology. He argued that the apostles were sent as preachers not sacrificers, and when the apostles established churches they appointed again preachers, teachers, and pastors, never sacrificing priests (I Tim. 4:13; I Tim. 3:2–13; II Tim. 4:2). There was no mention of the mass in the Acts. There we read of sinners converted, miracles performed, sermons delivered, churches founded; we see the Church gathering for Scripture reading and prayer; we read of controversies with opponents. Luther argued that Scripture clearly taught that Christ's sacrifice was offered once only for all time (Heb. 7:27; 9:25–8; 10:1–12), and that it was Christ who made the sacrifice, not man. He further argued that the dogmas of transubstantiation and the mass had no early patristic support, but were indeed a late development of the ninth century reaching formulation at the Fourth Lateran Council, 1215,[1] enforced by excommunication, imprisonment, torture, fire.

A still worse feature of this mischievous doctrine of the mass was that it begot the idea of purgatory or at any rate chose it as a partner. Purgatory was (and is) taught as some kind of intermediate state between heaven and hell. It is meant for those people who need further purification before they enter into heaven. Who knows, asked Luther, anything about this place? It is opposed to faith. The Gospel clearly teaches utter forgiveness and acceptance in Christ now: Who needs purgatory? Who first taught it? What more does a man need than to be 'in Christ', and the faith that nothing can separate him from this love? When all this theology was associated with the selling of indulgences for money Luther's spirit could contain itself no longer, and he posted up his Ninety-Five Theses in 1517 to

[1] Conc. Later. IV. Can. I.

discuss the scandalous imposture with his academic colleagues. This spark was a conflagration in weeks, and the whole of Europe was aghast that a friar of Wittenberg could stand up against the Church, and were dumbfounded when he asked the pope why if he could free these countless souls from torment for money he did not do so at once without payment.

Once the hollow falsity of this theology was exposed the echo of the priestly chains as they fell to the ground reverberated throughout Europe. There stood up, when once this word was proclaimed, a mighty army, free in the spiritual priesthood of all believers. This delivered men from the vague fear of the clergy. They realized there were not two orders of being, spiritual and lay, but one Gospel, one justification by faith, one status common to all men, clergy and laity alike. The difference lay only in the office God set a man to in life—father, scholar, farmer or pastor.

This principle of the priesthood of all believers is perhaps more responsible for divided Christendom than is generally considered. All subsequent attempts at reunion between Rome and Reformed religion have foundered on this rock, and it would be unrealistic not to give it due weight. It is not possible to over-emphasize the importance of the simple, striking, significant silence of the New Testament that priestly mediation is no part of the Christian ministry: and further there is not a single word to justify the secular power of prelates and priests. The priest is not a mediator between God and man, but only the servant of the Word. Neither can he play the role of prince.

It was in 1520 that Luther addressed the priests of the Church in his *Babylonian Captivity of the Church*, which was a dagger at the heart of the doctrine and practice of the Roman priesthood. The priests were scandalized by his open and unequivocal attacks on the magical character of the sacraments as then administered. To Luther the sacraments were outward and visible signs of the proclamation of the Gospel, an assurance of God's mercy in Christ, and a promise of His good-will towards

22

man. They were a gift of God to man, not an offering of man to God, never a means of effecting something magical by sacred formulae of sacrificing priests. The central act of Romanism, the mass with its miraculous production of Christ, the cultus by which Rome was Rome, was assailed and it has never been the same again in Christendom. There was no longer any place for a sacrificing priest, and no meaning to the indefensible traffic in paid masses for the dead. Yet what is important to remember is that all this came not from an enemy but a loyal priest who was and remained a high churchman and a sacramentalist. He believed in the real presence, but dismissed transubstantiation as heathen and idolatrous syncretism.

JUSTIFICATION BY FAITH ALONE ③

If the first principle of salvation in Christ alone apart from any works or merits of man meant the collapse of the mediatorial sacrificing priest, then together these two principles meant justification by faith alone. Faith in this context is often interpreted as a work, even by Protestants, in that it is sometimes understood as man's contribution to this new relation between God and man. This is not what the New Testament meant by faith nor what the Reformers taught.

Luther distinguished most carefully between what he called x2
historic faith and true faith. Historic faith meant the belief that Christ lived and that His teaching was good: it was no saving knowledge of Christ, the sense of Christ 'in us and for us'. Nor did he mean faith as a kind of assent. Faith was that which began with the working of God in us and on us, the calling of us out from where we are and where we are going to a new life and a new way. It begins with God, and this divine activity in a man, sometimes in mercy, sometimes in wrath but always re-creative and redemptive, is the power of God that authenticates belief. This means that a man is justified in the sight of God not by what he does, but by what God does in Christ. It is this

work he appropriates to himself. He knows that it speaks to his condition: he knows that it is redeeming him: the experience of the work is its own proof. It is this sureness and certainty of God's work that calls out the faith and trust in a man. It is an act of God (Eph. 2:8), but not only an act, a never-ending activity.

Justification by faith needs relating to justification by works. Paul sharpened the Gospel-Law tension on the grounds that Judaism had rejected Christ and with Him the Gospel. Christ before him had been in open controversy with the Sadducaic priests and Pharisaic rabbis because they rejected Him as the Messiah and as the fulfilment of the Law. They would not have a salvation of the free mercy of God to men as sinners all, but sought to maintain their God-given Law and Jewish religion. Christ taught that no man was acceptable to God, not even devout and good Jewish men (for example, Nicodemus in John 3), and only as penitent men reborn of God could God make his ways known to them. There were two wholly different views of man's salvation involved here. The Jews refused the Gospel as the end of the Law, and therefore could not see that "the Law in itself is an evangelical dispensation proleptically fulfilled in the Gospel": they lost the meaning of both. The Christian man saw the meaning and permanence of the old dispensation of the Law, was made aware of its fulfilment in the Gospel, and therefore came to respect both and to hold both together. Paul the rabbi pointed this tension in his evangelical missionary work so that men should see that a man cannot make himself acceptable to God by straining to keep the Law and its works: he could only be saved (even only know God at all) in his redemption by faith alone, apart from the works of the Law.

The issue in the Reformation was other than that, though the same principle. The issue then was not a contrast between justification by faith and justification by works, for the word 'justification' has a different meaning in the two usages. A man who knows he is justified by faith is saying not that he is justified at all but that God of His mercy had reconciled him, sinner as he is and sinner though he is. The man who claims to be justified by his works believes that he is acceptable on the ground of his works. At the Reformation the real opposite to justification by faith was the belief that forgiveness and acceptance were accorded on the ground of priestly absolution. This was the form of the issue then, and is much more the issue now.

To clarify this. Medieval theology had largely lost the powerful evangelical theology of Augustine with its emphases on sin, grace, the bondage of the will, and the predestinating sovereignty of God. It had to a large extent lost the gentle evangelical emphases of Aquinas in favour of Scotus. To the latter the process of justification had come to mean an infusion of grace which created a better habit of mind to God and man, and caused man's will to perform meritorious acts. These acts made him a better man: he became good by doing good. The necessary grace was infused at baptism and further 'shots' were subsequently supplied in the eucharist to keep a man going. But in practice the result or the process was marred or broken by sin, and therefore, the whole system of justification was set right again in penance, by which discipline and sacrament a man was once more restored to grace. The brevity of this makes the description rough and unfair, but it is near enough to the theory and practice of the time to show why half of Christendom went Reformed.

Luther had been through the whole process over the years with a zeal and faith that impressed his seniors in the order. He found in the acid test a bitter hollow uncertainty. He realized a man could go through the whole medieval process and never know the pardon and forgiveness of which the Gospel spoke. It dawned upon him with abysmal horror that the Church had lost or at least forsaken her ministry of the means of grace as established by the Apostles. Faith did not lay hold on the absolution of the priest: it lay hold only on what God had done in Christ for us. Luther was fighting for a true faith over against false ideas of faith: he was fighting for a faith in Christ alone in contradistinction to a faith based on the priest and his ministrations. There is born in a man a tremendous liberation when he sees that he is justified by faith in Christ alone, and knows what it is to have a heart hid with Christ in God. This experience of justification by faith alone was not used as a weapon against the Church or against the clergy: it was the norm or criterion a man might expect of both.

The reader should guard against thinking that this doctrine of justification by faith is a kind of one-sided emphasis of Luther and some evangelicals. Nor should he think of it as an item of doctrine of lesser or of greater importance. It is the groundwork of all doctrine on which alone any doctrine can be built: it is the basis of the Gospel we preach. It is incontrovertibly the meaning of the New Testament: 'by the deeds of the law there shall no flesh be justified in his sight: for by the law is the knowledge of sin' (Rom. 3:20). 'A man is justified by faith without the deeds of the law' (Rom. 3:28). 'Therefore being justified by faith, we have peace with God through our Lord Jesus Christ; by whom also we have access by faith into this grace wherein we stand and rejoice in hope of the glory of God' (Rom. 5:1-2). 'But Israel, which followed after the law of righteousness, hath not attained to the law of righteousness. Wherefore? Because they sought it not by faith, but as it were by the works of the law. For they stumbled at that stumbling-stone' (Rom. 9:31-2). 'They have a zeal of God, but not according to knowledge. For they being ignorant of God's righteousness, and going about to establish their own righteousness, have not submitted themselves unto the righteousness of God. For Christ is the end of the law for righteousness to every one that believeth' (Rom. 10:2-4). Or again: 'Knowing that a man is not justified by the works of the law, but by the faith of Jesus Christ, even we have believed in Jesus Christ, that we might be justified by the faith of Christ, and not by the works

26

of the law: for by the works of the law shall no flesh be justified' (Gal. 2:16). 'No man is justified by the law in the sight of God, it is evident: for, The just shall live by faith. And the law is not of faith' (Gal. 3:11–12). 'Before faith came we were kept under the law, shut up unto the faith which should afterwards be revealed. Wherefore the law was our schoolmaster to bring us unto Christ, that we might be justified by faith. But after that faith is come, we are no longer under a schoolmaster' (Gal. 3:23–25).

This doctrine had never been completely lost in the church. It had been preserved and maintained by St Augustine in the Pelagian controversy, yet the medieval theologians had shown a marked disinclination to promulgate it. Ideas of merit had been explicitly or implicitly brought into the scheme, and what was worse, grace was identified with the sacraments. And then the New Testament idea of faith had come to mean assent to credal propositions.

It was natural that the divine offer of the Gospel should be tainted with human ideas of justice and righteousness and morality. Christ had warned us of this in the protest of the Elder Brother, in the protest of the Labourers in the Vineyard, in looking at God in terms of a moral accountancy. It is not only the Jews who rejected the Gospel in favour of a Law, but the natural man always tends to do the same, and the Christian Church has always suffered from this spiritual myopia. It is interesting, too, to reflect that when Tyndale introduced evangelical theology into England it was Luther's *Preface to the Epistle to the Romans* that he translated, a document which develops this theology with clarity and simplicity.[2] It is also interesting in this connection to reflect it was when this very same document was read before John Wesley in Aldersgate in 1738 that 'his heart was strangely warmed', and so began the mighty revival.

[2] *Tyndale's Works,* Parker Society, *Doctrinal Treatises,* pp. 483 ff.

There were (and always are) two effects of this teaching of justification by faith. The first was (unexpectedly of a view which apparently disparaged good works) an immense outburst of good works. The difference between good works done for merit and these good works was that the latter were the spiritual outburst of useful and proper works directed by the Holy Spirit in faith towards God and love towards men.

The second effect was the havoc it wrought on popular religion. It made saint-worship, pilgrimages, formal penances, pardons, indulgences, intercessory masses, chantries and all similar activities foolish and otiose. The new thinking knocked the bottom out of the popular cultus. It was not merely the abuses and superstitions attached to them. The very 'theology' on which they were based was now suspect. These activities took on the appearance of utter futility, concerned to build up some 'merit' which not only did not exist, but was plain contrary to the known meaning of Scripture and ordinary common sense.

It is at this point more perhaps than any other, and possibly because it strikes Protestants so harshly, that the gulf between Roman Catholic practice and Reformed practice seems at its widest. When a Protestant stands in a Roman Catholic Church on the Continent and sees the holy water, the shrines and candles, the images and pictures, the myriads of altars, the tabernacles, and what appear to be crowds of priests, monks, and nuns milling around, he is made strikingly aware of the *otherness* of the Catholic cult. He sees these good, devout, Christian folk and wonders why there is this gulf, and what makes them so alien in thought and practice. Do they knowingly want it this way? Have they ever heard evangelical preaching? Do we really know and understand one another? Quite certainly, in any real conversations we have it will have to be on this level that questions are put—and answered.

Luther believed, and with him all the Reformers, that God had spoken in the Scriptures. They further believed that God still continued speaking to listening and believing man in and through the same words that He had spoken to the prophets and the apostles. It was a personal revelation in which God spoke in love to man, and regenerate man heard and answered in faith. Scripture, therefore, within the Reformed tradition is of divine authority, for it is the Word of God. No belief and no practice can be justified that is other than, outside of, or apart from the clear Word of God. On occasion the truth may be expressed in a non-biblical word, for example, 'homoousion', speaking of Christ as of one substance with the Father. It may be expressed in non-biblical modes, as, for instance, in the Athanasian Creed. Nevertheless, these are biblical truths not extra-biblical truths: nothing is true or authoritative that is contrary to Scripture. Whatever else it may be, a statement must be nothing less than scriptural.

This emphasis wrought havoc less perhaps on the theology of the late medieval Church than on its practices. The essentials of theology remained, but in those places where the Bible was allowed to speak, Catholicism simply turned and fled the field. There was no defending the sacrificial mass and with that all the abuses of indulgences, masses for the dead, purgatory, prayers to the saints, and the related scandals. There was no defending the dual standards of a spiritual and a secular morality. There was no defending the centrality of the priest and the forcing of the laity into some inferior role on the periphery. All this disappeared like snow before the March sun.

It is unhelpful to speak as if the Reformation set up an infallible Scripture in the stead of an infallible pope. At that time Rome, too, accepted the authority of Scripture, and there was in principle no difference between the Reformers and the

Papists. But, whereas the Reformation set Scripture as the sole authority, Rome professed this regard in theory while in practice there were modifying principles which they sought to relate to this authority. Consider, in this respect, her appeal to Scripture. She used Scripture as a sort of warehouse from which she drew texts to submit in support of views and positions held on grounds other than scriptural. She did not sit under Scripture but appealed to it to support her. That was not all. Not only were the Scriptures hardly ever read, but when they were, they were interpreted in the four-fold sense of Nicholas of Lyra, namely, the literal, the spiritual, the anagogic, and the analogical senses.[3] Nobody really knew where they were or what the Scriptures meant. Further, faith at this time was all too often conceived as assent to propositional statements about God, man, soul, grace, and other doctrines, and not in the biblical dynamic sense at all. Medieval theology had had the undesirable effect of placing the Church (in the shape of opinions of the Fathers confirmed by popes and councils) in between the believing man and his Bible in the same way as it had interposed the priest between the sinner and Saviour.

It was not only that the placing of the Bible as the ultimate authority in the Church swept away all the abuses, but rather that it made a new and stronger and Reformed people of God, strong in faith and strong in doctrine. As the Reformers had all found that God had spoken to them in the Bible, so all who

[3] This fourfold method of exegesis was a technique to bring out the meaning of Scripture. Not all parts of Scripture could be made to carry four meanings, but most did. The literal was the plain, grammatical, historical meaning. The tropological was the moral meaning, the evangelical sense made relevant to the individual. The allegorical was the interpretation it was made to bear for the Church as a collective whole, the sense that all religious experience is ecclesiastical experience. The analogical interpretation emphasizes that all our truths are partial and are part of eternity where all truth will be ultimately given. The technique, though quaint, should not be underestimated: it succeeded in quarrying a great deal from a given passage.

heard, poet and peasant, farmer and fisherman, people and priest, began to experience that self-authenticating authority of the Word of God. They heard the Father's voice, intensified their faith in His promise, and learnt afresh the work of Christ. The Reformation did not make them less church-minded but more, not less spiritual but more, not less catholic but more. They found new visions of the mighty great catholic purpose God had for His Church from Abraham on, and went through a liberation that was little short of thrilling when they discarded their priestly tutelage for the freedom wherewith Christ had set them free. They found faith less a mere propositional assent and more a growing commitment to God's promise in Christ, a promise plain for all to read and hear. Scripture was less a text-book of doctrine and morals: it was a plain account of that glorious experience of the men who had heard God and obeyed in faith, with the parallel warning of what happened to those who would not hear but chose their own way. When the common man had the Bible in his head, heart, and hand, he knew more about God's salvation than all the popes and cardinals, creeds and councils, priests and friars of all Christendom, because he had God speaking to him in his everyday life there and then. Indirect testimony of this was given by the protest of Luther's great opponent Eck who deplored the situation Luther had created in the words, 'Things have come to a sorry pass when even women answer back doctors of theology by quoting the Bible at them!' It was not that the Reformed man loved his Church less, but God the more. When a Church leads a man to God, the man loves his Church the more. All this amounted to a rediscovery of Scripture. It was less a revelation of intellectual formulae, more a communication of God with the reader. This word of God was recognized and authenticated by the internal testimony of the Holy Spirit.

Luther did not identify Scripture with the Word of God: N Scripture was the conveyance of the Word, the swaddling clothes which enveloped the Word. The authority belongs to the Word of God rather than to the Scriptures. Scripture is the Word of God insofar as it teaches Christ and leads to Christ. The man of faith knows that the Scriptures contain the Word of God, which, because it is God's, is ultimate and infallible. Nevertheless, he leaves himself as large a room as is necessary when he comes to assess the work of critical scholarship. It is not a matter of faith, nor does it improverish the Word of God, to study carefully the variant readings and to arrive at textual conclusions on how often a given text might have been edited or re-edited. Calvin did not allow himself the liberty Luther took; nevertheless, the letter had to be interpreted to the believing heart by the operation of the Holy Spirit.

It was this view of Scripture that compelled the Church of Rome (as it then came to be, unfortunately) to reconsider her position with regard to Scripture. At Trent she argued the authority of Scripture, certainly; but alongside, and of equal authority supplementing and interpreting Scriptures, she set Tradition. In a collection of essays by Roman Catholic and Protestant theologians called *Christianity Divided* Josef Geiselmann raises again this problem in a debate with Oscar Cullmann in the light of a new situation.[4] He points out that it was an Anglican called Palmer[5] who argued (though how he could do so he cannot tell for the full text was not then published) that the decision of Trent ought to be interpreted as the Anglican Church interpreted this relationship in Article VI on the sufficiency of Scripture—that is, that Scripture contains all things necessary for salvation. Palmer did not object to tradition which concedes that, nor presumably does Anglicanism.

In the light of this discussion, and on consideration of what actually transpired at Trent, it is quite certain that the sufficiency of Scripture was not maintained, nor was the view that authority rested on the 'partly-partly' relationship, namely,

[4] KÜNG, BARTH, CULLMANN and others: *Christianity Divided* (London, 1962), pp. 43 ff.
[5] William Palmer, 1838.

partly in Scripture, partly in Tradition. Geiselmann argues that nothing was decided at Trent on the relationship of Scripture and Tradition. He shows that the 'partly-partly' view was the first intent of the members at Trent and quotes the draft of the decree of 22 March, 1546. He shows that this was overwhelmingly approved by a large majority of the Council fathers. Only two, the learned Bonucci and the biblical scholar Nachianti, protested vigorously against this 'partly-partly' view. Consequently, a week later there appeared a modified text for the decisive session. There the 'partly-partly' had been replaced by the simple word 'and'. This means a clear decision not to be committed to the 'partly Scripture, partly tradition' view, but to leave the matter as Scripture *and* Tradition. This is an enormous break-through. If Rome allows herself to be persuaded that she cannot add to or deduct from Scripture in the matter of doctrine, but that Scripture is alone authoritative, then there is no objection to looking at tradition in the sense of comment or clarification. There is no indication that Rome is thinking this way. In fact Küng, one of her most 'advanced' thinkers, expressly denies the view that Trent is a deformation, and all Roman Catholic theologians known to the writer refuse to go back on Trent.

CHRISTOLOGY

It was argued earlier that Erasmus' theology was centralized on his doctrine of man, an emphasis which led him to think of Christianity in terms of man and his works rather than in terms of Christ and His work. It was this difference that separated the scholarly, cultured Erasmus from Luther with his total experience of conversion and redemption in Christ only by the mercy of God. It was not unlike the difference between Pelagius and Augustine at the turn of the fourth century: neither spoke the same language. Erasmus was a good man. He saw the corruption and worldliness of the Church, the intellectual jungle of its theology, the folly and absurdity of its practices. In this situation he sought to remove the corruption in high places and folly in lowly places and to simplify Christianity into the moral essence of the Sermon on the Mount. This was obviously laudable, but Luther interpreted everything differently. Starting from his total conversion in Christ he had nothing to preach or teach but conversion in Christ. Equally simple as Erasmus, he believed that the worldliness, the folly, the barren intellectualism were bad fruit from a rotten tree. He sought to make the tree good and believed that God gave the moral and intellectual and spiritual fruits.

Consequently, Christ filled the whole sphere of Luther's thinking. 'In Christ I have the Father's heart and will,' he said. Speaking of Christ he once said that it was as if a man had always known another man and had believed him a friend, but that in the hour of need it was proven, in that the other man stood in as a friend in deed. So much scholastic theology had been little more than conceptual and intellectual sophistry, and consequently the religious practice had been largely a matter of works-righteousness. Luther reached right back through the great fathers to the Bible and found his theology rooted in an experience of Christ, an emphasis on the redemptive and mediatorial work of Christ. He was Christ-centred and Christ-mastered. He could cry out at table, cry out in the open to the birds, of the mercy of God in Christ.

This is the reason he was so stiffly embattled against any worship of the saints, or any worship or invocation of the Blessed Virgin Mary. They were not colleagues of Christ, nor was Mary to be used as an 'easier' or 'more approachable' mediatrix. All Reformers insisted on the necessity of Christ alone for all believers, and also that Christ alone was the sole revealer of God and our only Mediator (and Advocate). True, Roman Catholics protest that they do not pray *to* the Virgin or the saints but only *through* them. It is a fair question to ask whether the rank and file of Catholicism believe and practice

34

this. Or more, to ask what the pope is saying when, on 24 January, 1965, in a speech on unity among Christians, he called the Virgin Mary 'Mother of Unity', and urged all Roman Catholics to pray to her for unity, asking them to give her that title in their prayers' (*Daily Telegraph*, London, 25 January, 1965).

It was and is this centrality of Christ in their theology that gave the Reformers and evangelicals such a sound sacramental theology. What was received in the sacrament was not some mysterious grace but Christ Himself, and therefore sacrament and Word must go together. The sacrament was a preached word of grace made visible, tangible. The Church of England unerringly set a sermon within the holy communion. Article XXVI expresses it: the sacraments are effectual because of Christ's institution and promise. In prayer and worship, alike in preaching and teaching, the Reformers see Christ as filling the whole sphere of God. It was a discerning comment when Harnack said of Luther that 'he joined hands with Athanasius across the centuries'.

THE CHURCH

There are two dimensions in the doctrine of the Church, seemingly irreconcilable, yet obviously part of the one doctrine. There is the Church in relation to God and the Church in relation to man. Or put more precisely, the Church viewed in its invisible and unknown relation to God in Christ, and the Church seen in its visible and known relationships to men.

The Reformers were uneasy in the identification of the Church of God with the Church men saw and experienced. They knew, as Augustine before them, that there were wolves in the pulpits as well as lost sheep in the pews, and it was in their doctrine of the Church that their new evangelical theology worked such far-reaching changes.

To them the Church began with God: it consisted of those whom God of His mercy had called out of a world under wrath, to whom he had graciously given His Holy Spirit. The type of the true churchman was Abraham who responded in faith not knowing whither he went. In fact, the whole story of the Old Testament, according to Luther, was the story of God's call to His people and what happened to those who did *not* believe, while that of the New Testament was simply the same story and what happened to those who *did* believe.

Luther viewed the Church as the communion of saints, called into existence by God and held together by His Holy Spirit, maintained under God by the proclamation of the Word of God heard and received in faith. It is a fellowship of Christian men and women whom the Holy Spirit has called and is sanctifying, who show their faith in God in love one to another. When asked once to define the Church Luther replied he could do it so that a child of seven could understand: those who hear the voice of their Shepherd (John 10: 3). The Church is, therefore, in one sense visible and in another sense invisible: invisible as to its divine origin and cause, visible as that fellowship where the pure Word of God is preached and the sacraments administered, and where faith brings forth the fruits of the Spirit.

Its ministry therefore is of these called and godly men set aside by lawful authority for this ministry to the people of God. They were men chosen, trained and appointed for this work. They were ministers to a congregation and in no sense mediatorial or sacrificing priests. Where the historic episcopacy was lost owing to the opposition of the prince or any other causes, the Reformers took the view that God was not limited by His priests. A minister can be called and sent to a congregation and not lose one crumb of the Gospel because he had not been episcopally ordained. The historic episcopacy is no part of the Gospel. It is both right and desirable to observe this where the tradition obtains, and where the Reformed tradition was officially allowed, but it is in no sense a *sine qua non*. Further, Luther took the view that, saving the essentials of the Gospel, it was a matter of indifference how a country chose to order its church life and government. Calvin, coming later, had to effect a precise church order to safeguard the Gospel, yet the same principle holds true; it is essentially the ministry of the Word and sacrament to a congregation of believing men. Apostolic succession meant a succession of true apostolic doctrine, not a matter of sees and bishops.

4. A MOVEMENT WHICH INVOLVED
THE WHOLE OF
WESTERN CHRISTENDOM

A remarkable feature of the Reformation was that it burst forth spontaneously all over Europe, and where there was not spontaneous combustion, it took only a spark to create a great blaze. We cannot recount that story here, we must remain firm by our task to make clear what the theological principles of the Reformation were. Nevertheless, it must be clearly stated that the Reformation was not a squabble between Luther and the pope, but represented a movement that gripped the whole of Western Christendom in its concern to have Christianity.

Zwingli

Independently of Luther, Zwingli (1484–1531) carried through the Reformation of Switzerland. There were marked differences between Luther and Zwingli: the latter was more humanist, more socialist, more liberal, but less theological. Nevertheless, he was entirely at one with Luther in his criticism of the theology and practice of sixteenth-century Christianity on the one hand, and with the essential evangelical emphases on the other. Zwingli thought Luther too conservative a reformer, had a much 'lower' view of the sacraments, had a different view of the relation of Church and state, and was given to the non-theological Erasmian view. Nevertheless, as the Colloquy at Marburg (1529) proved, except for their doctrine of the presence in the communion, Wittenberg and Zürich belonged to the same movement, and stood four-square on the same evangelical emphases.

Calvin

By the same token Calvin (1509–64) was of the same school. Forced to leave the University of Paris in 1533 for his Lutheran views, he settled in Basel, a town already reformed in 1517 under Capito and Oecolampadius, and when he arrived, peopled by Erasmus, Myconius, Bullinger, and other Renaissance and Reformed scholars. Here he published his *Institutes* (1536), and at once was compelled to take over the Reformation in Geneva. Calvin could be said to have been forced to take command of the Reformation army after Luther had recruited it.

In Geneva he faced his master problem. How could the Church be made not simply an institution for the worship of God but an agency for the making of men fit to worship him? He established a theocratic regime. He realized that the Reformed faith could live in a democratic city only by an enlightened pulpit speaking to enlightened citizens, and that an educated ministry needed an educated laity. He created both.

Nevertheless, in all the basic theological drives of the Reformers he stood in total agreement. He had certain differences of approach which issued in certain differences of emphasis, but he was always an evangelical. For instance, he did not (as Luther) approach God in the painful search of finding a 'gracious' God: God approached him. Therefore there is in Calvin's theology unmistakeable emphases of the sovereignty of God. Calvin felt mastered by God, that his will was now God's to deal with as He needed. He was God-mastered, God-possessed, God-intoxicated: Calvin's theology arises from this passionate theocentrism.

As an outcome of this was his emphasis on the hopeless corruption of man, and God's work in election and predestination, of His mercy and not of man's merit or effort. This dogma was a direct challenge to the claims of authority and finality by Rome in setting the determining issue in the objective fact of God's eternal decree in Christ and its certainty in such a full personal assurance of salvation, and not in the decrees of an all too corrupt Church. This issue is certainly one which we shall all have to face again if the ecumenical movement is to go forward.

Calvin held, too, the same high doctrine of Scripture. Scripture to him was inerrant, in that no more was included than was required, and no less given than was needed. It was also sufficient in that all that was required was in the Bible, and therefore, all that was in the Bible needed to be known. The Scriptures revealed all that a man can know about God, and all that he must know. Nevertheless, Calvin stressed the urgency of not seeing this as some kind of passive assent. There must be a change of heart and mind before approaching the Scriptures, and a concomitant submission to allow God to give us a right understanding through the internal testimony of the Holy Spirit. In regarding Scripture as this self-authenticating unity Calvin was providing an authority beyond conscience, reason, or the secular power, all of which could err.

When Calvin came to re-think an evangelical doctrine of the Church there were three conflicting conceptions. For his part he thought a visible organized society must show forth the principles of the true and Reformed religion. The constitutive principle to Rome was the hierarchy. To be a Christian was to be in communion with Rome, the guardian of truth and of morals. With this Roman view there had grown up a rather ill-defined view whereby this authority was closely allied with the civil authority and in fact superior to it. Luther saw the true Church as the elect of God, a community which was in essence invisible (though manifest to the world), and which had for its head Christ alone. The visible Church he viewed rather as a pale reflection of the true Church, and the seat of authority he rested not in a hierarchy but in the prince (or civil authority) as *summus episcopus*. The Anabaptists rejected both of these views. They proposed a Church gathered out of the world, a society of the redeemed, keeping itself pure by excommunicating those who failed to obey its rules, and repudiating any and every relation with the state or with secular society.

Calvin accepted none of these but took over elements of all three. With Luther he wanted to emphasize the true Church as invisible and that its constitutive principle was the Augustinian conception of the Church as the elect of God. With the Catholics he held that the visible Church is of vital importance; but argued further that it must show forth the principles of Reformed religion and have a definite though independent relation to the state. With the Anabaptists he insisted on a rigorous public discipline of all members of the visible Church while rejecting their idea of a 'gathered' community. Calvin would not separate the elect from the visible Church as a distinct community, but saw the Church rather as an objective fact given of God. He sought an independence of the state in the government of her own affairs yet made the highest demands on the temporal authority.

Calvin held, too, a high doctrine of the sacraments, though it was sane, sensible, and simple, and in accordance with Scripture. He thought Rome had vitiated her doctrine with suptleties, Luther was little better, and Zwingli had deprived them of their value. He defined a sacrament as 'an outward sign by which the Lord seals on our consciences His promises of goodwill towards us in order to sustain the nakedness of our faith' (*Inst.* IV, xiv, 1). But it is not in the sacrament that confidence should be placed but in the God who gives them: their substance is Christ. A sacrament had no meaning without faith, and a sacrament did not minister a kind of grace different from that received by faith. The efficacy of a sacrament arose from the Holy Spirit and the Word. The sacraments do not cause or effect anything: without the Word they are dumb.

41

Calvin upheld infant baptism as normative, on the grounds that it ratified to pious parents God's promises of mercy as well as introducing the child to the Church. Though essential, he held that baptism was not invariably indispensable.

It was in relation to the Lord's supper that Calvin showed fresh approaches. He joined issue with Luther on his so-called 'consubstantiationalism' (not Luther's word). Luther believed that Christ's body was 'ubiquitous', which meant that it was present 'everywhere', without limits and without limitation. It was from this principle of the 'everywhereness' of Christ's body that his sacramental theology developed its 'consubstantiationalism', which meant that the body of Christ was 'in, with, and under' the elements.

Calvin joined issue on this doctrine of the *mode* of Christ's present existence, but it must be said in defence of Luther, Calvin did not see the meaning of Luther's word 'body'. By 'body' Luther meant *Menschheit*,' in other words the humanity or 'human-ness' of Christ. All that Luther was arguing was that what we have to do with in the eucharist is the eternal ubiquitous Christ as incarnate for us men and for our salvation. Calvin set the body in heaven. He argued strongly against any idea of the flesh and blood of Christ being physically projected into man, but rather saw the divine activity as light (or sunshine transfusing its substance into fruit, as he once expressed it). Calvin nevertheless believed that we have the 'whole Christ' (*totum Christum*) and have Him dwelling in us. Luther and Calvin are nearer than they knew. Their real difference lay in their understanding of the present existence of Christ's humanity: Calvin localized it in heaven, Luther gave it the omnipresence of deity.

With Calvin the Reformation movement was finalized and systematized. We have seen in him the completion of Reformation theology. There were other Reformers, of course. There was a long line of them in Switzerland. Bucer of Strasbourg worked out the Reformation there, with wide influence elsewhere, on principles that combined both Lutheranism and Calvinism. Denmark, Sweden, and Norway all had their national reformers. Holland, too, Scotland and England. But the important thing for this book is to consider how Rome reacted to this movement and what happened in England, and to that theme, Part Two of our story, we now turn.

Part Two

HOW CHRISTENDOM REACTED

5. THE ROMAN CATHOLIC ROAD

THE POPE'S 'DREADFUL MISTAKE'

Writing in his definitive work on the Council of Trent, the Roman Catholic scholar, Hubert Jedin, speaks of 'the dreadful mistake' Pope Leo X (1513–21) made in regard to the Reformation. 'The fire of a religious revolution broke out in the house before its inmates were aware of it. Those who had watched the approach of the calamity and had endeavoured to arrest its progress were no more, while those who sought to put out the conflagration lacked the necessary strength. For more than a century and a half men had devised plans for a reform of the Curia and the Church. It had been discussed and written about, but never had a liberating step been taken by which the Papacy would have placed itself at the head of a movement for the Church's renewal. A grand opportunity had been missed.'[1]

What was wrong with the Papal Curia that for nearly two hundred years she resisted the promptings of the Holy Spirit? The views of the Reformers as set out in Part One of this book should strike any man as right and reasonable. To resist them or repress them could but spell division and disaster, for the Holy Spirit cannot always be blocked: He breaks out, and leaves His Church divided, but that is the price of having Him at all. If we all refused His activity we would be left with a human society or institution such as the Rotary Club or Free-

[1] Hubert Jedin: *Geschichte des Konzils von Trient* (Freiburg, 1949), definitive English translation by Dom Graf. Vol. I, p. 137 f.

masonry. The fact of our divisions means that at least we are not *all* deserted: He is still with us in our tensions and differences. Let us respond: let us wait on Him.

At the end of the fifteenth century and the beginning of the sixteenth the urgent and compelling need for a Reformation of the Church was recognized by all thoughtful men of Western Europe. It was expressed by everybody everywhere except by the papal Curia. Scholars and noblemen, parish parsons and monks recognized that the corrupt papacy was the running sore of Europe. They complained of clergy who did everything except care for souls. They complained of high clerical absenteeism. They wanted to restore the high morality of an earlier medievalism beginning with the bishops right down to the monks and nuns, yet what could they do when Cardinal Wolsey (to choose an English example) was arranging for his illegitimate daughter to be made Abbess of Salisbury? Further, humanism wanted to restore sound scholarship and rid the world of the sophistries of scholasticism. Many men (John Colet, for instance) felt that the Church had gradually lost all vision, even religion itself, and many felt that the urgent need was for individual man to rediscover religion, set himself in some proper relationship to God, and let Him purify the mind and conscience. It is interesting to reflect that Wycliffe, most Germans one hundred and fifty years later, Cranmer, and countless others, felt that the only way to relieve the Church of the load of evils under which she was groaning was to subordinate herself to the secular powers.

Leo X's 'dreadful mistake' was all of a piece with what had been happening long enough. The contemporary historian Guicciardini (1483–1540) gives us a remarkable insight into the way in which men realized that it was all wrong, yet sought to perpetuate it in their own interests—not unlike slavery later. He wrote, 'So much evil cannot be said of the Roman Curia that more does not deserve to be said of it, for it is an infamy, an example of all the shame and wickedness of the world.' Yet he continues to support it, saying: 'No man dislikes more than I do the ambition, avarice and effeminacy of the priests, not only because these vices are hateful in themselves, but because they are especially unbecoming to men who have vowed a life dependent upon God . . . Nevertheless, my employment with several popes has forced me to desire their greatness for my own advantage. But for this consideration I should have loved Luther like myself, not to free myself from the silly laws of Christianity as commonly understood, but to put this gang of criminals under restraint, so that they might live either without their vices or without power.' [2]

Had the papacy been intellectually aware of its weighty responsibilities, and spiritually competent to effect anything at all, the entire Reformation (save for the extreme left-wing fanatics) might have been contained within the Catholic structure to cleanse it and strengthen it. If ever the papacy betrayed Christendom she did in the sixteenth century. That dark hour hangs over Christendom as the hour of Judas hangs over the new Testament.

REFORMATION IN SPAIN

We should recall that it was the Curia that failed rather than the Church, which had never been without witness. The Church as a whole was very much alive to the need of a reformation, though some parts of Christendom saw the remedy in terms other than Luther's. For example, Spain showed how a medievalist may reform his Church. Spain believed that a measure of secular control was essential to set the Church in order. She revived her old canon law to control the corruption of the clergy. She gave a qualified support to humanism and at the same time reinstated scholasticism. She also sought a ruthless repression of heretical views, and at the same time, unqualified

[2] Quoted, *Preserved Smith: The Age of the Reformation* (London, 1920), p. 373.

support for the hierarchy and the rites and usages of the medieval Church. It was not a case of political men using the Church for their own purposes: it was rather a kind of regulative zeal not imposed but desired by the whole community. Perhaps in no place in Christendom was there this kind of religious unity between rulers and ruled as existed in Spain.

Isabella and Ferdinand steered a steady course ably assisted by Cardinal Mendoza, Fernanda de Talavera and by Ximenes. The latter, a devout Franciscan monk of humble birth, was elevated to the dignity of Archbishop of Toledo (1495) and effectively led his clergy in the ideals of St. Francis. Once having restored a noble and dignified morality to the rank and file of his clergy he sought to educate them by removing the ignorant and establishing schools of theology and new universities. The theology was a fresh study of Aquinas and the cutting out of Scotism and Occamism. He developed in his Thomist studies those evangelical and Augustinian features of which Luther deplored the loss. Biblical theology was developed, the New Learning encouraged.

The worst side of the Spanish reformation was the Inquisition. Everything contrary to the current ideas of revived medievalism was relentlessly crushed. There was no allowance for any new ideas, only the requickening of religious life within the framework of medievalism.

There was much in Luther the devout Spaniards appreciated at first, but it was their conservatism and medievalism that turned them against him. Here lies one of the illuminating shafts of light on the dark tragedy of the Reformation. It was in the excitement of a Spanish reformation of the kind sketched above that the young Emperor, the future Charles V, grew up. His tutor, later to be thrust on the throne of Peter, Adrian VI, unsuccessfully attempted to force a reformation on the whole Church on the lines of the Spanish reformation. There is further evidence that Glapion, the father confessor of Charles V, interposed when Luther was on his way to Worms and argued (with some imperial authority) that the young Emperor wholly desired a reformation and if Luther would hold his hand, he would bring it about on the lines of that which had happened in Spain. Others were saying the same thing elsewhere in Europe. Luther would not now turn aside and went to Worms.

Here three forces met in 1521: the German movement for evangelical Reformation championed by Luther; the Spanish reformation championed by the Emperor; and the appallingly stolid, stupid inertia of the Roman Curia whose spokesman was that awful Aleander. Tragically, the latter prevailed. Charles saw that unless Luther submitted to the kind of reformation which had happened in Spain, he would be compelled to oppose Luther. Charles with Luther (suitably modified) could have brought Rome to her senses: as it was Charles had to condemn Luther. The two reforming movements represented by Charles and by Luther clashed, and the Curia gained time and advantage. The reformation went on different lines and eventually took the form of a Counter-Reformation.

Charles almost succeeded when he contrived to have his old tutor, the reforming and righteous Dutchman, Adrian VI, made pope (1522—23). For the first time in one hundred and forty-four years, and never again since, a non-Italian ruled in Rome. Righteous, scholarly, utterly free of the sycophant nonsense about papal inerrancy and papal infallibility, he sought to reform the Church as Ximenes might have done. Pope and Emperor were now in utter harmony. For that matter many Italians were delighted when he undertook to cleanse the Augean stables.

The papal Curia was filled with dismay when the Holy Father camped contentedly in a corner of the palace with a homely Flemish peasant cook to look after his simple needs. All his reforms meant drying up rivers of revenue: humanists, clergy, lawyers, hangers-on, all realized like vultures that they could not pick dry bones for long. Adrian's programme might almost have been taken from Luther's *Address to the German Nobility*. But he was baffled, thwarted, and defeated at every point, and welcomed death as the only way out of an impossible situation. The unrepentant Curia killed him: the tail was wagging the dog. When the Curia suffocated Adrian, the hopes of reformation embracing the whole Church died: the world was left with a *Roman* Catholic Church on the one hand and *Reformed* catholic churches on the other.

REFORMATION IN ITALY

The other important country in reaction to the Reformation was Italy. But Italy presents a complex picture. There were three main groups: country folk, town folk, and the educated upper class. Her peasants were poor, illiterate, superstitious, and priest-ridden, almost pagan. Her town-dwellers were much more intelligent and religious, and realized that the cause of the malaise was the papal Curia. The outstanding writers and thinkers show a marked hostility to the Church, and saw it as a pawn in a political game worthless for the religious life. They, too, saw the need to reform the papal Curia but sighed at the hopelessness of the task.

There had been earlier unsuccessful efforts. Francis of Assissi had opposed to the growing materialism and worldliness of the Church the idea of renunciation and poverty, but his protest was drawn within and behind the papacy. Theologians too had been showing considerable criticism of the papacy, but they had capitulated to the mass conferences of Constance and Basel. Outbursts of popular discontent prophesied the disruption of the sixteenth century, and the greatest voice of all was that of Savonarola (1452–98), who appeared in Florence in 1489, fulminating against the sinfulness and apostasy of the time. Renaissance Florence was sympathetic, and when he tried to bring about his ends by political means, at first he succeeded with French help. This great puritan of Catholicism set up a

Christian commonwealth and sought by law to repress vice, frivolity, vanity, gambling, and all the social sins. His system proved impracticable and distasteful, and on the return of the Medicis he was brought to trial for sedition and error, convicted and burned, while professing himself a true catholic. Savonarola is sometimes described as a forerunner of the Reformation; but that is true only with regard to morals, not to theology. He was in no sense a theological reformer.

The great religious and theological issues that concerned a Luther, a Calvin, even a Teresa, seem lacking in Italy. To most Italians the Church meant the powerful institution at Rome with the pope at the head of its great hierarchy. The hopelessness of the picture made reforming men form little unofficial cells of reform. These reforming academies sprang up everywhere, consisting of pious men and women waiting and praying for the reform of the Church. The monastic orders were affected, too, and many of the Franciscans revived the ideals of their founder and were found preaching an evangelical theology akin to Luther's throughout the Italian villages, whilst the Benedictines appealed to the educated classes. The movement spread to the secular clergy also, among whom picked men of reforming tendencies were set to purify and idealize the ministry.

Hope of reform revived on the accession of Paul III (1534-49). He made Contarini, Caraffa, Sadoleto, and Pole cardinals, all four distinguished for their interest in genuine reform. A bull was published sketching the possibility of reforming the Curia. The four cardinals above, strengthened by five others, were commissioned to draw up a report on necessary reforms. This was presented to the pope in 1537, and a more scathing criticism of the state of the Roman Church could not have been written. It was so appalling that they dared not make it known, though a copy did reach Germany showing again how right Luther was. Reform of the Curia was pursued. The council called for Mantua, 1537, never met, for Charles and Francis were at war. It was postponed and called to meet in Vicenza. Charles would not accept a council on Italian soil, the pope dared not hold one on German soil. The pope pursued reformation of the Curia, Charles pursued his idea of settling the 'German question'. Contarini was allowed to meet the Lutherans to discuss the possibility of a council. The pope also sent Vergerius to Germany to discuss the details of the proposed council in 1535 (Vergerius was later converted to evangelicalism). Never were the signs more hopeful.

The Reformers, too, were pursuing a policy of rapprochement hoping for unity with Rome at the same time. The Lutherans lost the Swiss to their side in an endeavour to hold this possibility open, yet, in spite of great efforts by Bucer and Melanchthon, the cause showed no signs of failing.

Luther was never as enthusiastic as Melanchthon and Bucer, for not only was he more discerning, he had had an embittering experience. In 1518 Prierias had been ordered to conduct an enquiry, and adopted the foolish line that Luther was an ignorant heretic, and must recant. He argued that the pope was the Church and described him as the 'infallible judge of all controversies, the head of all spiritual, the father of all secular princes, the head of the Church and of the whole universe'. Luther, he asserted, was wrong in that he criticized the pope. Luther therefore was ordered to go to Rome within sixty days and recant of his heresies. The scholarly Cajetan had taken the same line at Augsburg, 1518, when he ordered Luther to recant, and asserted that the pope was above council, Church, and Scripture. John Eck at Leipzig, 1519, had argued for the authority of the pope and the infallibility of the Church. At Worms, 1521, Luther saw that Charles was to oppose him the moment he argued that the Church may err. Luther never thought after this that there was much possibility of making the Church of Rome reform herself on evangelical principles.

At Augsburg, 1530, when the Emperor had called a diet to

go into the division of Christendom, the Lutherans produced an eirenic and moderate statement of their theology. It summarized the essential Lutheran doctrines and reviewed the abuses demanding reform. The catholic party refuted this and demanded submission. They showed less concern for an evangelical theology, more for the authority of the Church. The evangelicals adhered to their protest of 1529 at Speier and to the Imperial Recess of 1526, whereas the Emperor promised a council within a year. At Nürnberg, 1532, both parties were enjoined to practise toleration until the matter could be discussed in council. Luther called all this 'muttering in the dark', and it is significant at this time how strongly anti-Roman were his writings. In fact he hoped for little more than political concord. In 1535 Vergerius adopted the old line of how could one fallible man, Luther, be right against an infallible Church. The Lutherans had consolidated their ranks and drew up the Schmalkaldic Articles (1537) where Melanchthon actually went so far as to say that he would be prepared to accept the papacy with modifications. At Hagenau (1540) a further attempt at unity was made but, unable to agree on any doctrine of the Church, the conference found it could make no progress and adjourned to Worms, 1540–41. Some progress was made, but the council adjourned to the Reichstag at Regensburg, 1541, when the Roman side was under the leadership of Contarini himself. Never had hopes been higher. Competent theologians on both sides, a genuine spirit of moderation prevailed. Some unanimity was found on the Augustinian doctrines of original sin and the bondage of the will. Agreement was reached even on the doctrine of justification by omitting the Lutheran *sola*. There was some division on the question of the power of the Church and a deadlock reached on the doctrine of the eucharist. The whole project was wrecked by the catholic insistence that a final decision rested with the pope. It was at this time that Luther said that Rome would have to change her teaching if any real progress towards unity were to be made. Within a year of

Luther's death the Emperor had actually taken up arms against the evangelical cause.

With Regensburg any hope of unity failed. Tragically, it was twenty years too late. When the good Contarini returned to Italy he found his influence had gone and died soon afterwards (1542), leaving a gap that none could fill. The Italians who had hoped to end division by agreement and compromise now realized there was little hope. The conception of a Catholic Reformation disappeared: the idea of a Counter-Reformation took its place.

CATHOLIC REFORMATION DISPLACED BY COUNTER-REFORMATION

It will be argued later in the book that the fresh hope in the present situation today (1965) is that Rome has done with the Counter-Reformation and stands in a position similar to that represented by many of the best catholic minds of the sixteenth century, such as Contarini, even Caraffa or Hermann von Wied, not to mention the religious such as Staupitz. God has in these days given us all a second chance, and both sides are four hundred years wiser.

Nevertheless, we need to be four hundred years wiser to be open to God's guidance in a new situation. There are all sorts of skirmishes on the periphery of the battle-ground—for example, the 'Honest-to-God' Movement and all sorts of 'parish and people' movements, and industrial and social experimentation. The main engagement has yet to be brought to a successful conclusion, though by now it takes an experienced campaigner to know who is fighting on which side.

It is therefore important to realize that it was the Counter-Reformation, a Catholic papist intolerant movement, that took the whole initiative of Catholic reform out of the hands of the enlightened scholarly spiritual men, who were yearning for a reform of the papacy and a refreshed theology to win again rebellious Europe.

IGNATIUS LOYOLA (CIRCA 1491/5–1556)

Ignatius Loyola, that fiery Spanish soldier, violently converted, is the mind and soul, even the genius behind the movement later to be called the Counter-Reformation. After his conversion, his total giving of himself to God, and after much travelling, his life's work crystallized out for him in middle age.

In Paris, 1534, Loyola chose nine disciples to work with him for the regeneration of the Church. They offered themselves totally and unconditionally to the service of the papacy in terms of service bordering on the extravagant. Loyola was a most devout and earnest Christian man yearning to bring about the moral transformation of his contemporaries. He sought to do this by offering to the masses a vision of the spiritual life of the standard of a Saint Catharine. He worked out his *Spiritual Exercises* to a refinement which produced a kind of hypnotic and ecstatic trance. He resigned himself, his mind and will, utterly and totally to a blind obedience to the Church, and with that compelling power that gripped the ancient mariner held everybody else to the same obedience and discipline, and, of course, the same mystic experience. He not only bound every soul to the unqualified duty of upholding medievalism exactly as it had always been—creed, custom, institution, even superstition; he not only exalted the medieval theologians to a parity with Scripture; he even went as far as to say: 'If there is something which seems white to us but which the Catholic Church defines as black, we must declare at once that it is black?'[3] The *Exercises* were the soul of the Counter-Reformation in the sense in which the *Liberty of a Christian Man* was the soul of Protestantism.

[3] *Regula* 13, p. 267. Antwerp Edition, 1676 (own translation).

Professor Leenhardt argues in a remarkable book [4] that there are two kinds of spirituality in Scripture, the Abrahamic and the Mosaic. The Abrahamic fulfils itself in the Pauline theology and becomes the characteristic spirituality of Protestantism: the Mosaic fulfils itself in Peter and becomes the characteristic spirituality of Catholicism. He makes a plea to see these two types of spirituality, not as history has made them, that is, as rivals, but what they ought to be, complementary. It is a thought as fascinating as it is enheartening. Certainly it was the Counter-Reformation that excluded the theological and biblical reformation demanded by the Reformers in favour of a re-formed medievalism. Equally certainly it has been this Catholic view of reform that split the Church into two even though it was the intention to unify it.

Loyola's three chief endeavours were to reform the Church from within, to preach the Gospel to the outsider and to the heathen, and to fight against heresy and schism in any shape or form. In Italy the beginning of a new order was founded in 1538. The ten associates travelled throughout Italy in a novel way, and in a novel speech, half-Spanish, half-Italian, preached a reform of morality from the top to the bottom. The good and liberal Contarini showed great friendliness to the reforming movement. By 1540 they had decided to form a new order called the Company of Jesus dedicated to the propagation of the faith and to the unconditional support of the papacy at any cost against all comers. They were a kind of 'salvation army' dedicated to serve the Catholic hierarchical church and to fight the enemy of God's Vicar with any weapon in the armoury. Nevertheless, salvation was a wholly different thing in the mind of the Reformers and in the mind of Loyola. To the Reformers it meant election by God and justification by faith alone: to Loyola it meant abject and unconditional obedience to the hierarchic church for only in total submission and obedience can a man grow virtuous. The weapons of the Reformers were

[4] F. J. Leenhardt: *Two Biblical Faiths* (London, 1964).

simply an open Bible, the weapons of Loyola the confessional and the directorate. Both roads may lead to Christ, but they are entirely different roads. The Reformers' way is the old original high-road with biblical backing: medievalism, even purified medievalism, has slender authority, if any.

This movement, by its zeal, devotion, and spirituality, not least by its appearance of being the traditional catholic way restored, attracted much interest and made considerable progress. It was easier to tidy up the house than to strip it and refurnish it properly, and this is how the biblical, evangelical, Protestant Reformation appeared to men in relation to the new movement of the Jesuits. Progress was made in Italy, Portugal, and Spain, less in France and Germany, which had had the benefit of Calvin and Luther. Faber, one of the original founder members, had by influence got himself on the Catholic team which discussed reunion with the evangelicals at Worms, 1540–41, but he was no theological match at all face to face with Melanchthon and Calvin, nor, for that matter, alongside his Catholic colleagues Eck and Cochlaeus. In fact none of them was a theological match for the Reformers. Luther realized that neither pope nor emperor desired a theological reformation, though Melanchthon, on the other hand, showed himself prepared to go a long way to meet them.

The Jesuits knew that the great enemy of the church in Germany was the scandalous lives of the clergy, and devoted all their energy to remedying this situation. Their strength lay in their uncompromising insistence that both clergy and people should go through a complete moral change, and, of course, still more, in that they themselves were men of pure spirituality and morality. The convert that effected most for them in Germany was Canisius, who with all the zeal and energy at his command made Germany his special care, and effectively managed to have the reforming von Wied driven out of his diocese at Köln at the moment when he was about to carry his whole diocese through a Lutheran Reformation. If von Wied had succeeded, the whole of Germany might well have gone evangelical. There was the added risk that as an elector he would have voted for an evangelical emperor.

There was also a further virtue in Loyola in his intense pastoral concern for people. In Italy he tackled with a will, and effectively, the three social curses of his time: the discarding of unwanted children, the ghastly institution of beggary, and the grave evil of prostitution. His views on this aspect of his work made moving reading.

It was the movement inaugurated by Loyola which not only won back a large part of Germany but which made the Reformation into Counter-Reformation, or in other words, made half of Christendom *Roman* catholic.

THE COUNCIL OF TRENT, 1545–63

The council finally met in 1545 in the village of Trent in the Tyrol. It's three main purposes were to overcome the religious schism, to reform the Church, and to call a united Christendom to crusade against the Turk. There were three papal legates. Giocchi represented the old guard and wanted no change. Cervini represented that large and growing party that wanted a reformation of life and character particularly among the clergy, but would make no concessions in doctrines, ceremonies, and institutions to the Protestants. They were uneasy about the possible consequences of the Spanish type of reformation in that it gave power to the state: they sought to increase not diminish the power of the papacy. Thirdly, there was the Englishman, Pole, a charming man of liberal outlook who sought reformation on the lines of Contarini at Regensburg in 1542, a view that was now virtually discredited.

The Council must not be thought of as some massive monolithic structure. There were serious cleavages of theological views (a mark of life within the Church as well as of the complexity of the situation). For instance, many Catholics saw

Luther as a scourge the Church deserved, administered by God, and saw, utterly rightly, that if the Church reformed her life and morals, Lutheranism would disappear. The Italians on the other hand tended to look to Rome to set things right. The Spaniards representing a third school thought the Curia so corrupt that only the secular arm could make a reformation possible. The Emperor, representative of a fourth approach, held the view that the differences between the Catholics and Protestants could be bridged, as he showed in his Interim of 1548. Only the Bishop of Trent saw things in the same way as the Emperor.

Cervini proposed that the fathers should define their theological opinions in relation to Protestantism, and while they were engaged on that the pope could be left to reform the Curia. Many disliked this negative anti-Lutheran policy of Cervini, and the Spaniards certainly would not accept the second possibility as remotely likely. The Bishop of Trent argued that a corrupt Church had produced Lutheranism and that Lutherans were brethren to be brought in, not excluded, much less attacked: 'Since the corrupt ways of ecclesiastics have given occasion to the Lutherans of fashioning false doctrines, then if the cause is removed the effect is more easily taken away. Far and away the best course will be to invite the Protestants themselves to the conference in a friendly and fraternal way so that they too may come to the synod and subject even themselves to reform.'[5] A thrill ran through the Council at these wonderful words but Cervini, in spite of the bishop's protests, persuaded the fathers rather astutely to discuss reform and doctrine together, knowing that sufficient heat would be generated in theological argument to make conciliation with Protestantism look too remote, and knowing too that the matter would be prolonged. The pope was alarmed to think that reform was even going to be discussed at all, but Cervini reassured him that the

[5] Theiner: Acta genuina ss. oecumenici concilii Tridenti, p. 40 (own translation).

Council would get nowhere anyhow, and that the Holy Father had no cause for alarm.

The Council fell into three main periods. Period I (1545–47), comprising sessions I–VIII under the papacy of Paul III (1534–50). Period II (1551–52), comprising sessions IX–XIV, Julius III (1550–55) being pope. Period III (1562–63), comprising sessions XV–XXV, Pius IV (1559–6) being pope.[6] For the purpose of this study significant selections only can be made.

The Council made no real doctrinal changes but it should be remembered that it removed a good deal of the Scotist scepticism which had troubled Luther, and in doing that made a fresh climate of thought. The fathers also worked in an atmosphere that had been created largely by humanism and Protestantism. Curialism, too, was now a potent force. These factors account for the fact that the theology of Trent is somewhat different from medieval theology and not the same thing as modern Roman Catholic theology.

In the third session the Council declared its Nicene orthodoxy and, most significantly, the Church was described as the '*Roman* church' ('*ecclesia Romana*').

Session IV saw the important discussion of the relative authority of Scripture and tradition, where after much argument the phrase '*partly* Scripture . . . *partly* Tradition' was changed into 'Scripture . . . *and* Tradition', a change of vital significance for the modern debate. There is no doubt that Trent wanted to place the authoritative exposition of Scripture in the hands of the pope, but that a powerful group prevented it saying so unequivocally.[7]

Session V discussed original sin. On first reading the decisions, the impression gained is one of rejection of Pelagianism and restoration of Augustinianism, yet closer study of this and

6 Consult Hubert Jedin, op. cit.
7 Jedin, op. cit., p. 87 *Küng, Barth, Cullmann*: op. cit., p. 43 ff.

the next, justification (Session VI), shows ambiguities which permit of semi-Pelagianism.

When the Council came to consider justification it was found that the fathers had to reckon with a strong force of catholic evangelicalism. Charles wanted them to steer clear of this: the curialists wanted to exclude Protestantism once and for all. Some Catholics wanted to accept the Lutheran view *in toto*: at this point the fathers came to blows! The New Thomists sought a modified Lutheranism but the Jesuit Lainez swayed the Council against this. As with the doctrine of sin, the decisions on justification begin nobly with splendid evangelical emphases, but before many chapters elapse we find them speaking of sinners 'converting themselves' and 'co-operating and assenting to the grace of God.' This was the touch of the Jesuit Lainez: they did not have a clue as to what the Reformers meant by faith, or grace for that matter.

In Session VII, when the sacraments were defined, transubstantiation was asserted, as well as the veneration of the sacrament and communion in one kind only. The Emperor was moved to protest again at this determined and deliberate exclusion by definition of his Protestant subjects, and when the members moved to Bologna to effect their Italianate idea of reform the more readily, Charles reacted violently so that the Council had to bring its sittings to an end.

The Second Period (1551–52) under the new pope Julius III (formerly papal legate del Monte at the first part of Trent), did not augur well. Hopes were raised of revising the first drafts and of reconciling the Protestants, but these expressions of hope were not met by deeds. The work was largely confined to the sacraments, no revised views were expressed, no pains taken to conciliate the Protestants. In fact, to read the anathemas is to read the Council as a protest against Protestantism. The decrees amount to the assertion that the usage and wont of the Roman Church constitute dogma, without regard to the plain meaning of Scripture, the plain meaning of the Fathers, and sound reason. None of the real issues Protestantism raised against late scholasticism are met: unmistakeably curialism and Jesuitism have gained the upper hand in the Roman Church.

When the anti-Protestant Caraffa ascended the papal throne as Paul IV (1555–59) there was not the slightest hope of the Council getting anywhere at all in its plans for the reconciliation of Catholicism and Protestantism. Reform was his job as pope, he said, not the council's. There was to be no tampering with the doctrines, usages, and institutions of the medieval Church. Heresy and schism were to be crushed by Inquisition and Index. Cardinal Morone found himself in prison, even Cardinal Pole was described as a heretic, and all who liked Pole were suspect. The days when Catholics could study Lutheranism dispassionately were now over; and it has remained like this until our own day.

Paul IV was succeeded by a very different type of man, Pius IV (1559–65), a lawyer not a theologian, and a realist. He realized that the Lutheran Church had now won political recognition, and that France was divided; Switzerland had gone; Norway, Sweden, Denmark had gone; England had gone and Scotland was about to go; Holland had gone and Bohemia, Hungary, and Poland were alienated. It is a marvel that none of his predecessors sensed this landslide, and in the hour of decision discussed things round the Vatican parish pump. He saw that unless the Catholic sovereigns and the papacy worked together against Protestantism, Catholicism could be disunited and crippled.

When the Council met for the third time it was not a council meeting to conciliate Protestantism but to reorganize the Roman Church. The new Emperor, Ferdinand, sought extensive measures of reform and had the support of the German Roman Catholics as well as the French. The Spaniards opposed any and every change in usage or doctrine. Nevertheless, all three wanted a reformation of the Curia.

Certain theological points were hardened. The eucharist and the communion were defined and the mass as a sacrifice defended. Certain regulations were made on matrimony, as well as on the government of, and education in, seminaries, the making of appointments and the like. Further, purgatory, the invocation of saints, the veneration of relics and images, and indulgences were all re-stated and defended.

Pius IV managed everything with the consummate (if not always commendable) skill of a lawyer: he kept up a majority of Italians on the Council to control all decisions, and at the same time worked patiently with all the Catholic heads of state to carry them along with him. Nobody, except the curialists appointed by the pope, liked this kind of government: one Spanish bishop protested he was made into a spectator. Nevertheless, the pope prevailed and also carried out quiet reforms at the same time, though on the final clash on papal supremacy he won by only seventy-one votes to sixty-six. Certainly, a very disquieting epithet constantly recurring in the decisions was the description of the church as the *Roman* Church.

Trent effected three things for the Roman Church. It provided a new look to doctrine: it removed many of the vagaries of late Scholasticism and at the same time set a stiffly embattled front against evangelical theology. It formulated afresh its own intellectual basis and on this established a proper hierarchy. It provided a system of gradual reformation which would eventually free the church from many of the evils which had contributed to the justice of the Protestant protest. It insisted on and made provisions for an educated clergy, a point at which all the Reformers had begun forty years earlier. It also made Catholicism into *Roman* Catholicism and anti-Protestant, largely owing to the influence of the Jesuits. Christian men would breathe more freely if Catholicism freed itself from its Roman and anti-Protestant bias and moved forward again into a free and biblical atmosphere.

62

In a thoughtful book [8] Senarclens defends the thesis that the trouble with Catholicism is that it is medieval and the trouble with Protestantism is that it is liberal. If the one could free itself of its medievalism and the other of its liberalism, he argues that there would be hope of a better rapprochement.

[8] J. de *Senarclens*: *Héritiers de la Reformation*, Vol. I, 1956. Vol. II, 1959. English translation in one volume: *Heirs of the Reformation*, 1963.

6. THE REFORMED CATHOLIC ROAD

THE REFORMATION IN ENGLAND

Characteristics of early British Christianity

The clear impression gained from a study of early British Christianity is of a Christianity that was scholarly, aggressively evangelistic, and ethical. The British monk Pelagius (c. 400), is found in vigorous argument with Augustine and others, prepared to justify his theology and ethics in Europe, Africa, and Palestine. There is enough evidence to show the concern of Pelagius for a moral and righteous society, as well as that his Church face the challenge of her own message. Augustine was theologically right over against Pelagius, nevertheless the witness of Pelagius is of inestimable importance. Two centuries later we see the British bishops very uncertain of Augustine of Rome when he came to Canterbury in 597. They resented his high-handed conduct, though eventually the British Church submitted to the Roman mission in 664 at Whitby. British missionaries spread the Gospel in large areas of Europe and it was of Bede that Charlemagne begged theological assistance, and in response to this appeal Alcuin of York was sent. When William of Normandy seized this kingdom he was obliged to depose our own Archbishop of Canterbury and his supporters, and to set in a Frenchman. There had long been a tradition of a British Church in these shores, possibly from the second or third centuries, the earliest known historical evidence (apart from a rhetorical phrase of Tertullian) being the posse of bishops who attended the Council of Arles in 314.

There had always been a measure of unease in England's relation to the papacy punctuated with occasional passages of arms, for example, with John and with Henry II. It was the fourteenth century that revealed how desperately sick Christendom was, and it was our own John Wycliffe (1324–84) more than anyone else who revealed it. There was the disgraceful Avignonese captivity of the pope which made of the papacy a corrupt vassal of the French crown. There were the wars in France which left England uncultivated, unmanned, poverty-stricken, and discontented. There was the ghastly Black Death of 1349. All these together made for a corrupt Church and a demoralized society. A strong anti-papal movement grew up and, in consequence, a strong anti-clerical movement.

Wycliffe, the 'evangelical doctor' as he was called, and the last of the great schoolmen, believed that a reformation would have to be *imposed* on the Church by the state, and that that would involve disendowment. He sought to de-secularize the leadership of the Church, and to evangelize its members. He developed a severe criticism both of the papacy and the clergy. He attacked their theology and he attacked their morals. He then sought to disabuse the Church of all its superstitions and evil practices. Towards the end of his life (1380) he attacked the doctrine of transubstantiation and the doctrine of the mass. He then translated the Bible, put it into the hands of his 'poor preachers', and sent them out to preach the Gospel two by two.

Almost the whole of the Reformation theology was on the lips of Wycliffe, but he was ahead of his time: he was two centuries ahead of the clergy, almost a millennium ahead of the laity. He had not the support of a strong enough king and did not win the support of the people. There was no printing press to spread his ideas. The movement was suppressed after his death and all theological teachers with Wycliffite sympathies were suspended at the University of Oxford. Comparing him with Luther, for instance, or with Calvin, we might say that the only real difference was that *mutatis mutandis* Wycliffe did not find it necessary to sharpen the issue into the doctrine of justification by faith alone, whereas it was the basis of all Luther and Calvin wrote and did.

Henry VIII (1509–47)

There were several factors favourable to reformation in England when Henry came to the throne. From the first he associated nation and Parliament with him in his actions and it was clear that the king not the church was to rule the country. The Renaissance era had brought with it the great explorations of Columbus and Vasco da Gama, new discoveries of science, the fresh printing of the classics, the art of the Renaissance, the break-down of feudalism with its rise of capitalism, all of which tended to make people feel that a strong hand to lead them through all these changes was demanded, particularly after the fatigue of the Wars of the Roses.

This period gave us Dean Colet (1467–1519) with his strong reaction against Scotism (even Aquinas, too) and his return to Christ and Paul, the Bible, the early Fathers and the Creed. Erasmus (1467–1536) found patrons in Warham and Fisher and friends in Colet and More; and where Colet had played havoc with contemporary religious practices Erasmus stepped in to oppose scholasticism and reduce Christianity to its first principles. Wolsey (1474–1530) was a conservative 'reformer': he began the suppression of monasteries, but he was a worldly prelate like all the rest and never desired doctrinal reform. He fell owing to his mismanagement of the 'divorce'.

The Reformation

The occasion was the divorce of Catharine of Aragon, but the cause was a resultant of many converging forces. For centuries there had been an anti-clerical movement not only against the worldly prelates but against pardoners, monks, friars, pilgrimages, and relics (see, for example, Chaucer's *Canterbury Tales*). There had also been an anti-papal movement of much longer standing. Then there had been Wycliffe's unanswered doctrinal revolt. At this time (round about 1528) the Church in England consisted of three main parties: the old adherents; adherents to the New Learning who had no sympathy with Luther yet desired a reform of abuses and worldliness; and the evangelical party, as yet with no leader, and its strength unsuspected.

When Henry failed to get the annulment of his marriage he embarked on an anti-clerical policy to curtail clerical incomes. He published an order for the destruction of all the heretical works of Wycliffe, Luther, Zwingli, and Tyndale. He accused the clergy of praemunire (the charge of recognizing papal jurisdiction in England), fined them heavily, took over the title Supreme Head of the Church of England, and forced from them an act of submission (1532). He embarked on his marriage to Anne Boleyn who gave birth to Elizabeth (1533). He pursued his anti-papist policy and was excommunicated in the same year. The next year saw the pursuance of the same policy, the outcome of which was a definitive breach with Rome. Then began a reign of terror in which men of the quality of Fisher and More were ruthlessly executed, along with many others, including the heads of monasteries. Henry dissolved the monasteries, the proceeds of which went not to the parishes and not to education, but to Henry and the greed of his confederates. Men do not gather grapes of thorns nor figs of thistles, and the closing ten years of Henry's reign were terrible indeed, when men ached under social, political, and religious grievances.

Nevertheless, those last ten years saw changes in religious faith and in certain formularies. At the instigation of Convocation the Great Bible of Cranmer was set up in every parish church in the land in 1538.

There were also the Ten Articles of 1536, mainly an effort to simplify Christianity and reduce it to its essentials. These Articles established the Bible, the Creeds, and the first four councils as the foundation of Christian doctrine. They permitted three sacraments: baptism, penance, and the altar. In the latter the real presence was insisted on but transubstantiation denied along with Lutheran consubstantiation and Zwinglian memorialism. Justification by faith was taught but rather on Melanchthonian lines allowing room for works. The worship of images and the veneration of saints were condemned. It was argued that rites and ceremonies could not remit sin. Masses for the deliverance of souls from purgatory were condemned. These Ten Articles, like everything else in Henry's reign, were nothing but a political move. They marked no doctrinal reformation but were rather a repudiation of papal supremacy. Melanchthon thought very little of them, even though they were drawn up in the hopes of a political alliance with the German evangelical princes, a move which went a step further in the Thirteen Articles of 1538.

In the same year Henry fulfilled his functions as 'Supreme Head' in the publication of *Injunctions* through Cromwell. First, the clergy were commanded to denounce the usurped power of the Bishop of Rome and to explain to their people the Ten Articles. They were to denounce excessive holy days. They were to forbid pilgrimages and not extol images, relics, or miracles: charity was better than gifts to images and honest work better than pilgrimages. They were to teach all people the Creed, the Lord's Prayer, and the Ten Commandments. They were to provide for education in the parishes and set up a Bible in every church. Provisions for the poor and the maintenance of the fabric were commanded. The clergy were ordered to teach and administer the sacraments more frequently, and to keep out of taverns(!).

An attempt to penetrate still closer to the heart of religion was made in the publication of devotional books. The first, *The Institution of a Christian Man* (1537), was drawn up by a committee of bishops at the request of the king. The book marked no advance in theology and reform, but was based on the Ten Articles. It contained an exposition of the Apostles' Creed, and also of the sacraments, retaining the pre-eminence of baptism, penance, and eucharist. It expounded the Decalogue, the Lord's Prayer, and the Ave Maria. It dealt with justification, purgatory, and relations with Rome.

Meanwhile orders were given for the destruction of shrines and superstitious images. Scoffing mobs jeered at the rood of Boxley complete with hidden wires for mechanisms for opening and shutting the eyes to delude the superstitious, and ribald ridicule laughed at what was but yesterday the Lord's own Blood of Hailes. Tombs and shrines were desecrated. Further Injunctions of Cromwell were issued (1538), doctrinally no different from the previous mixture. Apart from the setting up of the Bible in every parish church, Bible reading and preaching were encouraged. Pilgrimages, candles, beads, images, etc., were deprecated. A register of births, marriages, and deaths was ordered to be kept.

It is remarkable in how haphazard a manner Henry went about his business. His 'reform' began as a political movement, seemed later to be about to go doctrinal, but eventually went severely reactionary. He now forced through Parliament, staying himself and seeing that it was done, the Six Articles of 1539. His attitude now showed clearly that there was to be no doctrinal reform in England, even if Cranmer was at Canterbury. The Six Articles affirmed the doctrine of transubstantiation, declared communion in both kinds unnecessary, enforced the celibacy of the clergy, upheld monastic vows, and defended private masses and auricular confession. This was the triumph of unreformed views and shows Henry for the unredeemed catholic he was—as Luther always averred. The Articles were directed against any spread of the Reformation and were furnished with sufficient provisions for commissioners and heresy hunters to put them into effect.

The 'spiritual' counterpart of this was the *King's Book* (1543). This book was the revision of the *Bishop's Book* (1537) on the reactionary lines of the Six Articles. The King issued his own primer of devotion in 1545, after Cranmer had issued his now famous litany.

Edward VI (1547–53)

On the accession of the young King there was an instant clamour for reform, but the Protector Somerset left a good deal of responsibility in the hands of the cautious, moderate, kindly Thomas Cranmer. The Privy Council ordered all bishops to renew their licences under the new King, authorized the *Book of Homilies* (Cranmer's work), ordered the setting up of Erasmus' *Paraphrases* in the churches, and issued Injunctions denouncing images and ordering the gospel and epistle to be read in English.

Convocation decided on communion in both kinds and legalized clerical marriage. Parliament repealed Henry's treason and heresy acts, as well as his Six Articles; it enacted new laws for appointment to bishoprics, dissolved the chantries and converted the income into grammar schools and hospitals, and enacted the abolition of holy water, ashes, candles, palms, etc., as well as the destruction of all images.

A new order of holy communion was enacted in 1548. This was Cranmer's work, a compromise in an effort to carry along with him the bishops of the old learning. (The book was influenced by the liturgical efforts towards reformation of Archbishop Hermann von Wied of Cologne.) The book was legalized the next year. The marks of the new book were simplified services in the vernacular, an appeal to Scripture and primitive tradition, a universal congregational usage for the whole country, and the abolition of the mass as a sacrifice. Nevertheless, the book produced some unrest and rebellion.

Just before this Charles V had defeated the Protestant princes and issued his *Interim* (1548) to regulate religious matters in Germany. This produced a flow of scholarly Protestant leaders into this country, Bucer of Strasbourg, Peter Martyr the Italian, Fagius the German, á Lasco the Pole, and others, all of whom were given high ecclesiastical and academic preferment. These foreign Protestants gave some stimulus to the cause of Reformation. Cranmer in 1550 published his *Defence of the True and Catholic Doctrine* showing that the Reformers were seeking to reform Catholicism. When this thesis was resisted by Gardiner it was clear that the 1548 book would have to be rewritten. This was done with the help of the Continental Reformers (1552), followed by the Forty-Two Articles of 1553, later reduced to the present Thirty-Nine.

The young King was now dying. There were intrigues in the matter of succession. The country was in economic distress, the Church bruised, plundered, and torn, the universities were in a state of decline. Men were tired of this state of affairs and wondered if Mary might be the means of restoring peace to a distracted church and country. English folk were not happy with the foreign Protestants, they hated Northumberland and his ways, they needed a fresh start.

The Marian Reaction

But Mary (1553–58) had one concern, to restore a *Roman* Catholicism of the papal kind. There were three parties now: the Roman Catholics, the Protestants, and the middle party, which was anxious to restore the church's catholicism but not the Pope with it. If pressed to a choice this party would have preferred Rome to either Geneva or Wittenberg.

Mary first restored everything as it was in Henry's day acting with moderation on the advice of Charles V. Then, after her marriage with Philip in 1554, she revived all the medieval laws against heresy and repealed all laws enacted against the Roman See since 1529. Cardinal Pole was re-installed and had his glorious hour in giving absolution to a penitent assembled Parliament. Cranmer was found guilty of treason and burnt as a heretic, and when too a long line of men such as Latimer, Ridley, Hooper, Ferrar, Taylor, Rogers, totalling some three hundred, were burned for heresy, the people were disquieted. She further involved the country in war with France. When she died in 1558 she was execrated by her own people. It was all a tragic failure : circumstances of birth and upbringing, desperate divisions, and a personal failure of her own life proved too much. In some senses this unhappy and tragic figure was the best of all the Tudor dynasty, but her reign was a miserable disaster for the country and for Christianity.

Elizabeth (1558–1603) and the Elizabethan Settlement

To appreciate the work of Elizabeth we need first to appraise the dangers of her position. First, the sight of Germany ravaged with civil war, as well as France, in open strife of Catholic against Huguenot, made civil war a real possibility. Secondly, the Roman Church had reconverted itself to Christianity and the Counter-Reformation with its weapons of Index and Inquisition were real preventatives against evangelical thought and learning. The Jesuits, too, were militant. Thirdly, foreign states were hostile. Neither the King of France nor the fanatical King of Spain were prepared to stand by in idleness and permit a Protestant settlement in these shores. This hostility culminated in the Armada, 1588. Fourthly, Elizabeth was the illegitimate child of the disgraced Anne Boleyn : her title was most insecure, particularly with Mary Queen of Scots alive.

A new factor developed, Scotland. Hitherto Scotland's affinities had been with France, but under the ministry of John

Knox she turned her eyes to England. The Protestant settlement in England owed its safety to the victory of Calvinism in Scotland. In 1560 Elizabeth sent an army to Scotland to help them to expel the French garrison.

When Elizabeth turned her attention to a religious settlement she realized that most people were attached to old forms, and though the Romanists wished to return to the Marian settlement, the Protestants sought a settlement on the lines of the Continent, a policy that would have broken the continuity of the old English Church. The Queen was Protestant in outlook and uncompromisingly anti-papal, determined to be supreme in her own land. She settled her position in the Church of England as Supreme Governor (a *jus potestatis* not a *jus ordinis*), and settled the church's in an Act of Uniformity on the basis of the 1552 Prayer Book. She settled, too, the Thirty-Nine Articles, though she failed to make effective the *Reformatio Legum* of Edward VI. A royal visitation put all this into effect, as well as the denunciation of images and relics, the destruction of shrines and altars, pictures and paintings, and the encouragement of sermons and Bible reading. The Marian bishops who objected were simply deprived.

During Elizabeth's reign the country was in a parlous state. Spiritual destitution stalked the land: churches were in ruin; the clergy were few and many of them were dumb dogs; the universities were at a low ebb; the church, already over-plundered, could no longer support her clergy, and there was much episcopal absenteeism and clerical illiterary. Nevertheless, it was Elizabeth's faith, backed by many a good Englishman, that if she could but only preserve the peace, the intellectual and spiritual life of England would course back again, provided Romanism and Puritanism could be staved off. She sought a comprehensive settlement that would embrace the entire people of England. It was to be both Catholic and Protestant, but never papal. Catholic, in that it was built on the foundation of the Bible, the primitive Church and the Fathers: Protestant, in that it rejected the pope, transubstantiation, private masses for the dead, indulgences, communion in one kind, compulsory confession, celibacy, and purgatory.

This settlement, nevertheless, left the two main religious problems of Romanism and Puritanism as active and dangerous. The Supremacy Act of 1563 was not enforced until 1570, and even then the Romanists enjoyed a large measure of immunity. Some were imprisoned, some fined, but most were left unharmed. Pius V (1566–72) in his fanaticism made a false move. He knew that England was the key to world Protestantism, and in his ineffectiveness in bringing England to heel, foolishly excommunicated Elizabeth, absolved all her subjects from allegiance to her, and ordered no subject to attend an English church. Further, though many Romanists attended their own parish church (going secretly to mass as well), the extremists actually founded their own seminary in Douay to train priests to re-convert England, a body strongly buttressed by the Jesuits. This was to go too far. When the Romanists involved themselves in plots and political intrigue (the Percies and the Nevilles, 1569, the attempt to raise Ireland in revolt with the help of Spanish and Italian troops in 1579, and the plotting round Mary, Queen of Scots, 1579–81) there was but one end. The government enacted legislation on treasonable conduct, banished the Jesuits and clamped down on popish recusants. Nevertheless, many Romanists were sufficiently spiritually minded to hate the Jesuit intrigues to restore Romanism by foreign arms: many Romanists were loyal Englishmen.

In her endeavour to make the English Church co-extensive with the English people, Elizabeth found an obstacle of a different kind in Puritanism, though not the same political threat. Puritans were rigidly Calvinistic, marked by a stern morality, love of Scripture, and an awareness of God's abiding presence, and stiffly embattled against anything frivolous. There were the moderates and the extremes, but they did not seek to secede from the church, rather to control it and convert it to a purer life.

In its first phase, rather a Lollard phase if anything, they concerned themselves with public worship, seeking to remove all that was non-scriptural—for example, vestments, the sign of the cross in baptism, and the giving of a ring in marriage. Many of the theologically minded (Beza and Bullinger, for example), took a dim view of such triviality, advising conformity in such non-essentials and working for a theological reform from within the church.

In its second phase Puritanism was concerned with church government, the parity of ministers and the extirpation of prelacy as a relic of popery. They sought to presbyterianize the Church of England. They attacked the church for retaining popery, instancing the surplice, the Prayer Book, the ring, the sign of the cross, kneeling at communion, saints' days and the like, as well as the orders of bishops, priests, and deacons. Hooker was splendid in his reply. He argued that practices were not necessarily bad because they were observed by papists, and that Scripture must not be required to do what it was never intended to do. Reasonable customs will always be acceptable to reasonable men. They further attacked the church on the ground of its practical abuses—the lack of a preaching ministry, pluralism and non-residence, the scandalous lives of some clergy, the abuses of ecclesiastical courts, excommunication as a procedural method, the commuting of penance against payment, and archiepiscopal dispensation.

The programme of the Puritans was clear. They were to remodel the church on presbyterian lines: 'parity of ministers' was their cry, abolition of episcopacy their aim. The congregation was to call its own minister, who was to work with his elders and deacons, and the government of the whole was to be by synod. The Puritans were to bide their time until at an opportune moment they were to rise and take over the Church in England. Gradually Puritanism grew more extreme and more nonconformist.

The third phase was marked by a separatist tendency. Independence was now born, and its party cry, 'Reformation without tarrying for any'. This tendency rejected presbyterianism as well as the royal supremacy. They would not recognise the historic church as a church at all because it was contaminated with evil-livers, and thought of the church as consisting of saints. This party crystallised out in the Brownists who eventually fled to America on the Mayflower in 1620.

This controversy drove the Church of England to defend herself and define her position, a task assumed by Richard Hooker who wrote his *Ecclesiastical Polity*, 1594–97. He opposed the Puritans for their biblical literalism. He argued that the Church was an organic not a static institution, and that its government in any one particular country and its administration at any particular time must change according to historical necessity: therefore, the Anglican church possessed continuity with the medieval Church. On the same grounds he accepted the non-episcopal orders of Continental Protestantism: the succession had regrettably been broken, but apostolic succession he argued as a matter of doctrine not sees.

This was and has remained the definitive Anglican position. In respect of comprehension it finally broke down under the Stuarts, and in the Act of Uniformity of 1662, when Anglicanism was imposed upon the country by law and the presbyterians and independents were lost to the national church—a fact accepted by Parliament in 1689. Nevertheless, the Church of England stands by its Reformation formularies, its Articles and its Prayer Book, and in these the Anglican divines reformed the historic catholic church of this realm. Whereas Trent had given to Christendom *Roman* Catholicism pledged to the theology of the Counter-Reformation, thereby making Roman

Catholicism essentially anti-Protestant, England (and with it Sweden) gave to Christendom a *Reformed* Catholicism. This idea of Catholicism, wholly independent of the papacy, was based on Scripture, tradition, and reason, allowing all matters of government and administration to national custom and law.

Part Three

CHRISTENDOM'S SECOND CHANCE

7. REFORMED PROTESTANTISM IN CONVERSATION WITH A REFORMED CATHOLICISM

POPE JOHN'S ENCYCLICAL

There is now a new theological climate in Christendom since Pope John issued his encyclical of 29 June, 1959, calling the Vatican Council. As a consequence of this, Roman Catholic theologians have shown themselves prepared to discuss with Protestant theologians for the first time since 1555 the issues that rent Christendom in the sixteenth century. Rome has been prepared to confess her own sins and shortcomings, and Pope John has spoken of Protestants as beloved brethren separated.

ITS MEANING

More than this we cannot reasonably expect. It is enough for a beginning. Yet we need a sober realism in assessing its meaning. We must not see what is not there: we must see this from the Roman not the Protestant end. All the Roman Catholic leaders and spokesmen have been at pains to declare with Christian candour that they are not discussing reunion but unity, and that unity to them means an unconditional return to the fold under their chief shepherd, the pope.

In the sixteenth century Rome committed herself at Trent to an anti-Protestant position, a position she cannot repeal. There is not the slightest hope in the dialogue between Catholicism and Protestantism unless Rome can find some way of suspending the anathemas of Trent. Roman Catholic scholars open up no possibility of this. For example, Jedin, the authority on Trent, refuses to entertain a revision of Trent as a possible way of *rapprochement*. Cardinal Bea, the President of the Secretariat for promoting Christian Unity, appointed by Pope John and confirmed in his post by Pope Paul, expresses the same view, and argues that the teaching of Trent requires not reformation but completion. Cardinal Bea allows submission to Rome in matters of doctrine and discipline as the only way forward; no other course is conceivable. Our own Cardinal Heenan has expressed the same views in pulpit and press and on television.[1] Hans Küng allows *de*formation of theology in the history of the Church but argues that *de*formation of the Church's dogma is unthinkable, and that therefore there can be no place for 'reform' in this matter.[2]

Rome further demands not only submission to the pope, but the acceptance of the dogmatic decrees of 1854 (Immaculate Conception), 1870 (Papal Infallibility), and 1950 (Assumption of the Virgin Mary). It is futile for high Anglicans to think that there is some affinity with Roman Catholicism in their version of Anglicanism, an affinity resolutely repudiated by those they are courting. Newman, who knew both at first hand, argued that the Anglican and Catholic are two religions which are irreconcilable. Anglicanism cannot be dressed up to look like Roman Catholicism.

IS THERE A WAY FORWARD?

Roman Catholic scholars have always recognized that it is the evangelical scholars who are most aware of the gravity of the issues of the Reformation struggle. Evangelical theologians welcome the new spirit of conciliation, but acknowledge that

[1] See Philip Hughes' essay in Atkinson and Hughes: *Anglicanism and the Roman Church*, p. 26 f.
[2] Hans Küng: *The Council and Reunion*, p. 162 ff.

the essentials of the problem have not changed at all. Roman Catholic scholars and evangelical scholars are one in their candid refusal to minimise the theological doctrines that divided Christendom and keep it divided.

The present writer is of the opinion that some formula will have to be found to enable the Roman Catholic Church to return to the debate of the pre-Trent days, when so many of her scholars and her leaders hoped to answer Luther and to reform their own Church while *holding Luther and the evangelicals within the fold*. Luther was never answered, only condemned. As constituted, the present Vatican Council can never reconsider the issues raised in the sixteenth century, nor say that Trent was an unmitigated disaster for Christendom. Trent did not speak with a single, infallable voice: the fathers there were much too spiritual, much too godly, to pretend that the answer to evangelical theology was to anathematize it, and that the way to unity was to pack the Council with Italian yes-men. No one is asking Rome to say this, but evangelicals may properly say so. Therefore, is it not possible for a really competent trustworthy commission of Protestant and Roman Catholic scholars to be seconded by their respective communions, to meet together over a period of years, and to give Christendom a fresh appraisal of four matters? One, of the Reformation; two, of those men and movements who unsuccessfully sought *theological* reformation of Christendom after Luther's protest but before Trent; three, of the manoeuverings of Trent and its final decisions; four, of the whole ecumenical movement today.

There was before Trent a genuine possibility of the Church going *reformed* Catholic. Trent gave us admittedly a wonderful moral reformation, a not inconsiderable doctrinal improvement, particularly with regard to later scholasticism, but tragically an anti-Protestant commitment with respect to the great theological issues of the Reformation (discussed in chapter 3). These reappraisals could very humbly be offered to the Roman Catho-

lic Church and the Protestant Churches for consideration. Trent
adopted a position in an hour of controversy, a position which
need not be treated as fossilized formulae but as answers which
a living Church may re-express in more complete and less in-
adequate formulae in the light of the guidance of the Holy
Spirit. After all, Roman Catholicism and Protestantism are now
four hundred years wiser. A *repeal* of Trent is out of the
question, a *reappraisal* of Trent could be a godly and judicious
step, particularly if done by godly and learned men of both
sides. The problem in a nutshell is this: Can Roman Catholicism so reform herself as to take Protestantism into its system?

WHAT THIS MEANS

This would mean a profound and heart-searching examination
of historical and theological material carried through by the
highest academic standards and the purest spiritual purposes.
It would demand all the support of Christendom and a dis-
ciplined restraint to permit the Holy Spirit to drive the argument to its true conclusion. Both sides will be much hurt, both
much chastened. Only in this way can the Spirit speak to the
churches.

It will also mean an exhaustive discussion of the main Reformation issues discussed in chapter 3, to see if both sides
together cannot arrive at a more adequate and perhaps less
controversial method of expressing them. This will mean the
examination of the evangelical doctrine of salvation by Christ
alone apart from works or merit, and its relation to the Roman
Catholic scheme of redemption. It will mean a re-examination
of the doctrine of the priesthood of all believers and a re-
assessment of the role of clergy and laity in the Church: the
bitter attack on the mediatorial, sacrificing priesthood; the
whole doctrine of the mass, transubstantiation, masses for the
dead, purgatory, indulgences and the centrality of the mass in
Roman Catholic theology and practice. It will mean a re-

examination of the doctrine of justification by faith alone, a doctrine very nearly assimilated by Cardinal Contarini in his desire to reform the Church and retain the Lutherans. It will mean the re-examination of the Protestant view of Scripture in relation to the Tridentine view (not unequivocally expressed) of tradition as of equal weight with Scripture. It *is* of equal weight if it is genuine development of Scripture in a changing world, but Protestants will draw the line at dogmas which are added or deducted *de fide*. It will mean a fresh consideration of the doctrine of the person of Christ, and many harsh things will be said on the alarming Mariolatry of modern Roman Catholicism: none has written more sensitively on Mary than Luther, yet none more trenchantly on Mariolatry. Perhaps the doctrine of the Church will prove the hardest struggle, nevertheless, the hierarchic Roman view must be examined in the light of the purely biblical view of the Reformers.

The present writer is much enheartened to have read in recent years the remarkable works written by Roman Catholic scholars on most of these subjects, the profound debates by Roman Catholic and Protestant scholars in journals and paperbacks, the eirenic, hopeful, and cautious statements issued by church leaders to the press.

Let us consider these for a moment. Who could fail to see the importance of Hans Küng's *Rechtfertigung* (Paderborn, 1957) in which he gives a masterly account of justification by faith, and actually argues that he is saying the same thing as Karl Barth; or of his two remarkable books, *The Council and Reunion* and *The Living Church*? Or consider the Roman Catholic *Faith and Fact* series with one hundred and fifty titles by some of the finest Catholic scholars of Christendom all designed to explain the new spirit in Catholicism. Or, further, consider the remarkable debate in *Christianity Divided* where five great themes that divided Christendom are reopened and rediscussed by scholars of both sides. Scripture and tradition are discussed by Cullmann and Geiselmann; the Bible by Fuchs, von Ruler, and Michael Stanley; the Church by Barth and Weigel; the sacraments by Thurian, Oberman, and Schillebeeck; justification by Torrance and Küng.[3] It is not a mere wind of change but a veritable tornado.

A REFORMATION OF ANGLICANISM

At the same time Anglicanism must set its own house in order, and present both to Rome and the Free Churches a genuine Anglicanism based on a biblical theology; a sound catholic theology; a clear-sighted hold of the formularies, articles and Prayer Book; and an historical grasp of the last four hundred years—all integrated by sweet reason. This is our tradition and this is what we have to offer. This is what Anglicanism meant by comprehension: a clear stand over against Rome and an equally firm front against fanaticism and sectarianism. We dare not negotiate with Rome, nor with our Free Church brethren, until we equally have faced again the theological issues raised in this book.

But Anglicans must not be deceived at this point. The present writer suggests that the malaise of Anglicanism arises essentially from theological and biblical malnutrition. We all groan at an episcopal leadership working overtime to keep mere machinery from breaking down or courageously trying to stop Anglicans slipping off the raft they hope will drift somewhere. We all groan at the intellectual penury of our clergy and see standards falling abysmally low at a time when educational standards have never been higher. We all groan at a laity that hardly knows where it stands or what it believes on any theological or moral question. We are all aware of the disease, but it must be diagnosed before it can be cured or alleviated.

[3] Consult: Select Book List, p. 93 f.

The 'atheistic' and radical approach of the Bishop of Woolwich with his concern 'to begin at the other end' cannot bring in the reformation he rightly seeks, and can only cheapen Christianity. He stands condemned by the Reformers (and by his own Anglican tradition) who spoke of reformers of his sort as merely 'preaching man' ('*hominem praedicare*'). No mere technique can bring in anything, for we have nothing and are nothing. We can only offer the liberating language of biblical and classical theology concerning God and His mercy in Christ, delivered by men known of God to men in need of God, truths so clearly re-declared by the Reformers to Christendom in all languages of Christendom. Language of this kind breaks through any church and any society. Such theology would set men in relation to God as well as to the world they live, and restore the historic and catholic mission of Christianity to secular man. A recovery of this sort would make Anglicanism fit to have conversation with a fast reforming Romanism.

Equally clearly must we be done with any flirting with Rome. Our high-church brethren keep up a pretence that Anglicanism is very near to Rome in its theology and practice. There is not a single Roman Catholic scholar who would endorse that view, for they are too well aware of the differences, even the cleavage. They respect an evangelical and understand him; they never can get to grips with the Anglo-Catholic for they cannot accept his position. Logically he belongs to Rome and they cannot see why he has not got the sense to see it. Roman Catholics may be hostile to Protestantism, may not understand it, but they know that it is a force to be reckoned with in that as long as it exists it is a condemnation of the catholicism they profess.

CHURCH MORE THAN THEOLOGIANS

Lest we ever forget that the Church does not consist of theologians in discussion, and that such discussion is fruitless if it does not speak to the condition of the ordinary layman living his ordinary life, we can also be glad that the movements we have been discussing are stirring the churches, not only the theologians of the churches. Recent trends are showing that the Roman Catholic layman is reading his Bible and looks there for the authority of the Word of God as it is evolving in a living Church. This is a sounder view of Scripture than exists in some Protestant circles which look upon the Word as something quarried out of Scripture and tend to fall into the danger of seeing it as an ancient oracle rather than a living Word. It is anachronistic in Roman Catholic circles now to counterpoise Scripture and tradition. This liberating view eases the problem of infallibility, in that a Roman Catholic may now not claim that the last word has been spoken say on transubstantiation but, rather, that whatever more is said will not be *less* than that doctrine sought to preserve.

Then there are important doctrinal emphases coming out in the liturgical movement. The Church means the people nowadays rather than the clergy: the Church is almost a lay movement that has a few priests for liturgical and pastoral purposes. The Roman priest is now almost a minister to the people— at any rate, in a Roman Catholic kind of way. Central terms and ideas, for example, grace, transubstantiation, even the Trinity, under the scrutiny of logical analysts are undergoing remarkable changes of depth and emphasis. Most striking of all are the great changes in moral questions. The Roman Church in view of its more educated laity seems prepared to grant great liberty of conscience. It is seeking new ideas on the training of the clergy. It allows laymen to write as experts in their own field. It has even conceded in principle that it has been wrong in viewing birth control as necessarily against the natural law. These, and many other changes, encourage an observer in his view that there is a real movement of the Spirit abroad.

Men will always feel strongly in matters of religion yet must be free to express themselves. Further, controversy is not always harmful, for much clearer views may emerge as a result. Nevertheless, mischievous and misrepresentative propaganda will do no good. Men look for informed discussion and debate, and will accept no less. Propaganda tends to rely on grotesque practices or views which are idolatrous or blasphemous (and which no informed observer wants to defend anyway), and some controversy rages round peripheral rather than central ideas. If we are in controversy, we must discuss the real differences between us, such as Christ's saving work and how it is appropriated, and not abuses which nobody defends, nor use names such as 'Babylon', 'the mother of harlots', and the like which are not conducive to clear thinking.

At the level at which the discussion of this book has been maintained there is no room for cheap debate. Nevertheless there is sufficient of it abroad to suggest terse rebuttals of the charges that are sometimes made against considering the Church of England as the true catholic church reformed in this realm.

It is argued that Anglican clergymen are not validly ordained, and in practice 'converts' to Roman Catholicism are 'baptized' again, make their 'first' confession and their 'first' communion, on the assumption that Anglican clergymen have been offering invalid sacraments on the authority of invalid orders. Yet, when Cardinal Pole returned to this country in the days of Mary he did not reordain all the priests who had received orders in the reigns of Henry VIII and Edward VI by the English Ordinal. Another form of misrepresentation of this same objection occurred in the reign of Elizabeth when Roman Catholic propagandists spread a story that Archbishop Parker had been consecrated in a public house and neither his orders, nor in effect those of almost all the English bishops and priests, were valid orders. Even Leo XIII (1896) returned on slightly different ground to the theme of discrediting Anglican orders.

It is also argued that the Anglican Church was founded by Henry VIII. Yet Henry VIII lived and died a Catholic: he limited the powers of the papacy in England by acts of Parliament, because the English people at that time found the papacy in practice a political foreign power. Any historian knows that the Catholic Church existed long before Rome assumed its leadership, and that acknowledgement of papal supremacy was not for centuries a condition of membership of the Catholic Church. To the Roman sneer, 'Where was your church before Henry VIII?' the old reply of Adams is worth making: 'Before the dayes of Luther . . . an universall Apostacie was over the face of the world, the true Church was not then visible; but the graine of trueth lay hid under a great heape of popish chaffe' (*Works*, p. 556).

Another form of this same charge is that the Anglican Church committed schism in breaking away from Rome. Yet the Church of England maintained its continuity with the Catholic Church in all essentials: ministry, creeds, sacraments, Scriptures. It unchurched no other church: it asserted the ancient right of reforming and revising its worship and discipline and to remove practices in conflict with Scripture and catholic tradition. It was Pope Pius V who in 1570 excommunicated Elizabeth and called upon her subjects to dethrone her. The plots to assassinate the Queen and to bring in foreign Catholic invaders to force England into Roman Catholicism were Catholic inspired. If Anglicanism was schismatic, why wait till 1570 to say so? Was she not schismatic before that?

It is also argued that in the thinking of Anglicans the sovereign is head of the Church of England, and it is asked how a layman can be head of the Church. In Henry's Act of Supremacy he sought to deny to the pope the headship of the Church in England, and was granted that title with the saving clause 'so far as the law of Christ allows'. Queen Elizabeth took the title of Supreme Governor in 1559, and since then this has been the title and responsibility of the sovereign. The sovereign possesses no rights in the church: the sovereign cannot ordain, or change doctrine or practices. The crown cannot even *make* bishops: a bishop can only be made by election and by consecration of other bishops. The sovereign may regulate the services of the Church but only through Parliament, which represents in government the interests of the whole English people and therefore of the English church. The King or Queen of England is no more supreme over the Church of England than Constantine when he presided over Nicea in 325 as 'bishop of bishops'.

The plea of the present writer is to be done with such fruitless controversy and to turn in harmony to the really knotty problems we have inherited these four hundred years.

The argument of this book has been to look at the theological principles of the Reformation that divided and divide Christendom. All of these are valid, scriptural, catholic truths. To defend herself the Church of Rome eventually took the wrong road at Trent by choosing the path of Counter-Reformation and anathematizing Reformation theology, excluding these principles from Catholicism and leaving Protestantism to maintain them. It was a failure of nerve under duress. These truths cannot be jettisoned with impunity. In the changed situation of today the present writer makes a plea for Rome and Protestantism to go behind Trent to Augsburg, 1530, and collectively make a reappraisal in the light of four hundred years of history.

Evangelicals cannot accept Roman Catholicism as it is, nor can they accept an idea of unity which compels them to repudiate biblical theology. Catholics cannot accept Protestantism as it is. Can they not together under God retrace the principles for whose truth godly, scholarly Christian men not only sacrificed unity but their life rather than lose them; together thank God for preserving them these four hundred years; together wait on God to show them how and on what terms He can make them one? Both sides shall then emerge differently, but nothing true shall be lost.

QUESTIONS FOR GROUP DISCUSSION

Part One

1. Do you think the theological issues of the Reformation are dated?

2. How do you understand the fundamental concerns of evangelical theology?

3. Do you think these concerns were embodied in our Anglican formularies and Book of Common Prayer?

4. How far do you think that the malaise of Anglicanism is due to a loss of its evangelical and biblical theology?

5. Can the occasion of the Reformation be differentiated from its cause?

6. What do you think of the view that the crisis for Christianity lay in the *Aufklärung* of the eighteenth century and not in the Reformation of the sixteenth century?

7. Are the theological principles of the Reformation communicable to modern secularized man?

8. Is the current missionary movement concerned with the Reformation at all? Is the European crisis of the sixteenth century of any significance for an African or Asian?

Part Two

1. Why do you think the cause of *Catholic* reformation was lost to the cause of *counter*-reformation?

2. Why is Catholicism *anti*-Protestant?

3. Is Protestantism a protest against errors or a witness for truths?

4. What explanation would you offer of the change of mood in Roman Catholicism?

5. Do you feel that the Elizabethan Settlement was in the interests of Evangelical theology?

6. Do you hold with a national, established church?

7. Do you think that Elizabethan comprehension, based on Scripture, tradition, reason, is tenable?

8. On what principles would you relate Church and state?

Part Three

1. Has Pope John's Encyclical more than a Roman Catholic significance? Is Christendom afforded a 'second chance'?

2. Is it possible to begin the debate behind Trent?

3. Is there any sense in describing evangelicalism as reformed Catholicism?

4. On what lines would you want to see a reformation of Anglicanism? Does our hope lie in the 'new reformation' of the Bishop of Woolwich, in parish and people movements, or where?

5. Would you recommend some truce to propaganda, and the elevation of the debate to appropriate biblical, theological, and spiritual levels?

6. How would you suggest the Church of England could restore the idea of the layman as the centre of its doctrine of the church with the priest as his minister? What

dangers are there in professionalism or clericalism? What reforms are needed at parish and national level?

7. Is establishment a hindrance to the Church of England?

8. What subjects would be most profitable for study and discussion in an ecumenical movement at parish level?

SELECT BOOK LIST

A flood of popular literature on Vatican II is available in all libraries, and no attempt is here made to estimate it. Nor are standard works by standard scholars listed here. The list would have been larger than the book. The following is a selected list of books in English, readily available, utterly reliable, which may be consulted by the interested reader.

Karl Adam: *The Spirit of Catholicism* (old but good; Catholic), London, 1929.

J. Atkinson and P. E. Hughes: *Anglicanism and the Roman Church, London,* 1964.

Cardinal Bea: *Unity in Freedom* (authoritative), London, 1964.

H. M. Carson: *Roman Catholicism Today* (a first-rate account from an evangelical viewpoint), London, 1964.

G. Dickens: *The English Reformation* (excellent historical statement), London, 1965.

Faith and Fact Books: There are 150 volumes of varying worth. Some are brilliant. Numbers 134–9 on the Ecumenical Movement are germane to this book.

R. Fuller and R. P. C. Hanson: *The Church of Rome—A Dissuasive* (very good), revised edition, London, 1960.

Hubert Jedin: *A History of the Council of Trent* (classic, authoritative, Catholic), Edinburgh, 1961.

W. von Loewenich: *Modern Catholicism* (a Lutheran scholar with a sympathetic approach to Patristics and Catholicism), New York, 1959.

F. J. Leenhardt: *Two Biblical Faiths*, London, 1964.

A. de Mendieta: *Rome and Canterbury* (Benedictine converted to Anglicanism), London, 1962.

J. de Senarclens: *Heirs of the Reformation* (two volumes in one), London, 1963.

Stagbooks:

Hans Küng: *The Council and Reunion*, London, 1961.

Hans Küng: *The Living Church* (sequel to above), London, 1963.

Hans Küng: *The Changing Church*, London, 1964.

Hans Küng: *Structure of the Church*, London, 1965.

H. Küng, K. Barth, O. Cullmann and others: *Christianity Divided* (specially valuable), London, 1962.

Gregory Baum: *The Quest for Christian Unity*, London, 1963.

E. Schillebeeck: *Christ the Sacrament*, London, 1963.

J. C. Heenan, H. St John Bea, and others: *Christian Unity —A Catholic View*, London, 1962.

Vittoria Subilia: *The Problem of Catholicism* (excellent but difficult), London, 1964.

CHRISTIAN FOUNDATIONS

The first titles in this series are: